Made in Hawai'i

Made in Hawai'i

by JANE FULTON ABERNETHY
SUELYN CHING TUNE

illustrated by JULIE STEWART WILLIAMS

A Kolowalu Book
University of Hawaii Press
Honolulu

05   04   03   02   01   10 9   8   7

Library of Congress Cataloging-in-Publication Data

Abernethy, Jane Fulton, 1933–
    Made in Hawai'i.

    (A Kolowalu book)
    Bibliography: p.
    Summary: Instructions for craft projects and activities
which are traditionally Hawaiian. Includes how to use ti
and coconut; how to make tools, cordage, toys, and leis;
how to prepare foods and natural dyes; how to plant such
crops as coconut, banana, and sugarcane; and how to
play Hawaiian games.
        1. Handicraft—Hawaii.   2. Hawaii—Social life and
customs.   [1. Handicraft—Hawaii.   2. Cookery, Hawaiian.
3. Dyes and dyeing.   4. Games.   5. Hawaii—Social life
and customs]   I. Tune, Suelyn Ching, 1944–
II. Williams, Julie Stewart, 1928–   ill.   III. Title.
TT24.H3A24   1984   745.5   83–4895
ISBN 0–8248–0870–3

University of Hawai'i Press books are printed on acid-
free paper and meet the guidelines for permanence and
durability of the Council on Library Resources.

To
Padraic and Jerry
Stewart and Stacey
Faye and Anne
and to
Ellen Poepoe Stewart
Hung Leong and Mabel Ching

Contents

Foreword

The ever-increasing interest in Hawaiian culture has caused those involved in this subject to ask for more and more resource material. Persons who are skilled in research and writing are challenged to fill this need.

Among popular Hawaiian projects which have been neglected by writers are books of instruction explaining articles of a Hawaiian nature made from local materials. Observant people find an abundance of interesting plant and animal products not being used to the fullest, and often they express the desire to be able to convert these into ornamental and useful objects. Some wish to make articles for use in pageantry, to take on excursions, or to use in playing games. Some people would like to carry out activities to learn more about the basic nature of these materials. This book of simply written, explicit directions for adults and children to use in carrying out craft projects and related activities answers these expressed needs.

The authors of this how-to-do-it book, Jane Abernethy and Suelyn Ching Tune, are teachers of long experience at The Kamehameha Schools. They have presented the instructions through a vocabulary suitable for young and mature readers and for those with a variety of interests.

The materials needed to make the projects described here are readily obtainable and familiar to most island residents.

The tools needed for these activities are to be found in most home or school craft shops. We congratulate the authors for sharing with us a number of projects not discussed elsewhere.

The numerous illustrations by Julie Stewart Williams, also a teacher of long experience at The Kamehameha Schools, add a great deal to the book. Her clear, realistic sketches of the materials show the steps to follow in constructing articles and in carrying out various activities. A person with no craft experience may read the written directions, follow the illustrations, and complete projects that seemed, at first, to be complicated.

Those of us involved in the many phases of Hawaiian culture extend a sincere mahalo to these three talented instructors for researching, writing, and illustrating this attractive and useful book. We predict that many readers will become absorbed in carrying out these interesting projects and pleased with their finished products.

Me ka pono

Donald D. Kilolani Mitchell

Consultant in Hawaiian Culture,
The Kamehameha Schools/Bernice Pauahi Bishop Estate
and Research Associate in Anthropology,
Bernice Pauahi Bishop Museum

Preface

This book was written to provide easy-to-follow directions for anyone interested in learning a few of the ways Hawaiians used the varied and colorful materials in their environment.

We have included directions only for activities or crafts that require tools and materials readily available to and easily used by anyone at little or no cost. Activities that require a high degree of skill or special tools are not included. Further, except in the section on leis, the plants discussed in this book were used by the ancient Hawaiians.

Human resources were at least as valuable as the many references we consulted. We want to thank Ann Asakura-Kimura, Alison Chang, Mary Joan Gill, Kaiponohea Hale, Moses and Naomi Kalauokalani, Allen Kanoa, Ruby Hasegawa Lowe, Veronica Medeiros, R. Janthina Morris, Sarah Nakoa, Irmalee Pomroy, Violet-Marie Mahela Rosehill, Irene Thoene, and Stewart Nani Williams, Jr. for their help.

We owe special indebtedness to Beatrice H. Krauss, ethnobotanist and research affiliate at the Harold L. Lyon Arboretum of the University of Hawaii, who has been our teacher in many areas of Hawaiian studies and who was kind enough to review our manuscript and to check our illustrations for botanical accuracy. We thank Donald D. Kilolani Mitchell, consultant to The Kamehameha Schools/Bishop Estate in Hawaiian culture and research associate in anthropology at the Bernice Pauahi Bishop Museum, who also read our manuscript. His well-researched publications were of great help, particularly in the section dealing with Hawaiian games.

The *Hawaiian Dictionary*, by Mary Kawena Pukui and Samuel H. Elbert, was consulted for Hawaiian usage and spelling. We thank Robert Lokomaika'iokalani Snakenberg, education specialist in Hawaiian studies for the Hawaii State Department of Education, for reviewing our use of Hawaiian words.

In order to ensure ease of reading for younger readers, readability formulae (Dale-Chall, Fry) have been applied, but we hope this book will be useful to readers of many ages and interests.

I. TI (KĪ OR LĀ'Ī)

1. *How to Prepare Ti Leaves for Use (Kī or Lā'ī)*

Ti leaves can be used for many things. Often you need to remove the midrib, or bone, from the center of the leaf before you use it. These directions tell you how to do this.

WHAT YOU NEED

A fresh, green ti leaf.

WHAT TO DO

1. Turn the leaf so that the shiny side is down, or away from you.

2. Bite the midrib about five to eight inches away from the beginning of the stem. You could also use scissors or a knife to cut into the bone. Do not cut it all the way through. Do not make a hole in the leaf itself.

3. Now hold the leaf in both hands with your thumbs on both sides of the cut. Push up on the broken bone. Pull the top of the leaf down. Push and work the bone toward the stem. Peel this part of the bone away from the stem. Your ti leaf is now ready to use.

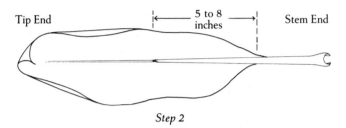

Tip End   5 to 8 inches   Stem End

Step 2

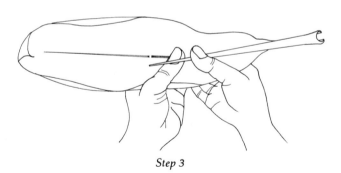

Step 3

1

I. TI (KĪ OR LĀʻĪ)
2. How to Dry Ti Leaves

When you are using ti leaves, try to pick only as many as you will need. If you pick too many, save the extra leaves and dry them. When they turn brown you can use them to tie lei carriers, to make cords, or to make sandals. You can find directions for making these things in this book.

To dry ti leaves, put the stems of about ten leaves together. Tie the stems tightly so they will not come apart as they dry and shrink. Separate the leaves from each other as much as you can. Hang the bundles with the stems up in a dry place until you are ready to use them.

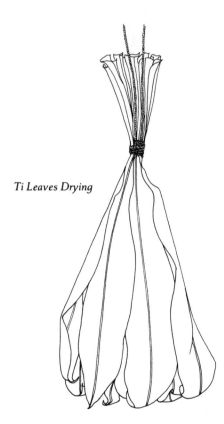

Ti Leaves Drying

2

I. TI (KĪ OR LĀ'Ī)
3. *Ti Leaf Lei (Lei Lā'ī)*

In old Hawai'i a ti leaf lei was worn by the *kahuna lapa'au,* healing priests or doctors. You can use ti leaves to make a lei like the ones *kahuna lapa'au* wore by following these directions.

WHAT YOU NEED

Two large, fresh green ti leaves with long stems.

WHAT TO DO

1. Take the midrib out of both leaves. Look at section I, 1 for directions for doing this.
2. Tie the stems together in a knot. Trim the stem ends a little to make them feel comfortable around your neck.
3. You can wear the lei just as it is. Or you can tear the leaves along some of the lines, or veins, in each leaf to give the lei a fringed look. Tear the leaves from the midrib out to the edge of the leaf. Start from the tip end of the leaf.

You can also make a lei using only one ti leaf. Tear a deboned ti leaf in half beginning at its tip. Tie the stem ends together. Then tear the leaf along the lines in each half leaf to give the lei a fringed look.

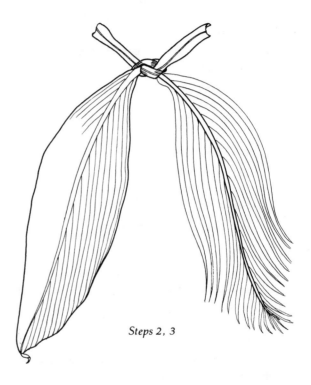

Steps 2, 3

3

I. TI (KĪ OR LĀ'Ī)
4. *Ti Leaf Cape or Skirt #1 ('Ahu Lā'ī or Pā'ū Lā'ī)*

In old Hawai'i a ti leaf rain cape was made of ti leaves tied to a net. You can make a smaller, simpler shoulder cape or a skirt by following these directions.

WHAT YOU NEED

1. About one hundred to one hundred fifty large, green ti leaves. The number you use will depend on how big your skirt or cape should be. Pick ti leaves with long stems.
2. A cord or string on which to tie the ti leaves. This string must be a strong one and long enough to go around your waist or shoulders. Add enough extra string so that you can tie it easily.

WHAT TO DO

1. Tie your cord or string between two chairs.
2. Take the bone out of each leaf. Look at section I, 1 for directions for doing this.
3. Split the stems in half, from the end of the stem up to where the leaf begins. Often when you take the bone out of a leaf the stem will split in two, so you will not have to do this to many of the leaves.
4. Hold the leaf in back of the cord. Have the side that is not shiny facing you.

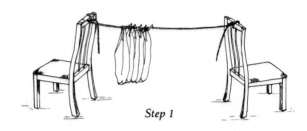

Step 1

5. Now bend both halves of the split stem over the cord.
6. Keep one side of the split stem down over the cord. Pull the other half stem back behind the leaf and across the first half stem.
7. Now tuck the stem half you are winding into its own loop.
8. Slide the ti leaf close to other leaves you have put on the cord. Tighten the knot by pulling a little on one stem half and then on the other.
9. Trim the stem ends when you are finished. Be careful not to cut the string when you trim the stems.

You can keep a hula skirt, or *pā'ū lā'ī*, wrapped in a damp cloth, in the refrigerator for two or three weeks. A rain cape, or *'ahu lā'ī*, will keep you dry even after it turns brown.

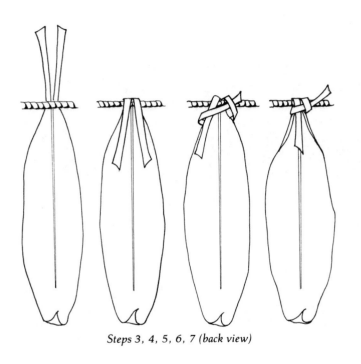

Steps 3, 4, 5, 6, 7 (back view)

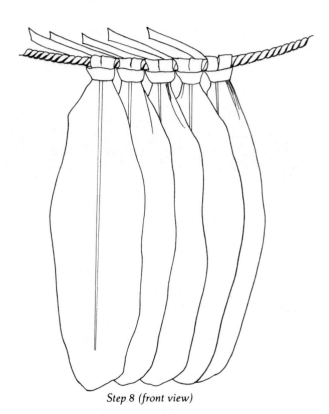

Step 8 (front view)

I. TI (KĪ OR LĀ'Ī)
5. *Ti Leaf Skirt #2 (Pā'ū Lā'ī)*

Hula dancers in early Hawai'i wore skirts made of tapa, or *ka-pa*. In later years they made hula skirts from ti leaves. The directions on this page tell you another of several ways to make a hula skirt using ti leaves.

WHAT YOU NEED

1. About seventy-five large, green ti leaves. The number you use will depend on how large your skirt should be.
2. A strong cord or string on which to tie the ti leaves. Make the cord long enough to go around your waist. Add enough extra string so that you will be able to tie it easily when your skirt is finished.

WHAT TO DO

1. Take the bone out of each leaf. See section I, 1 to find out how to do this. Be careful that the stem ends do not split in half when you take the midrib out.
2. Tie your cord or string between two chairs.
3. Hold the leaf in back of the cord. Have the side that is not shiny facing you.
4. Bend the stem over the cord.
5. Bring it to the left and pull it around behind the leaf.
6. Now bring the stem toward you on the right side.

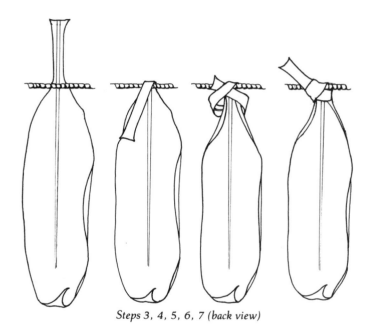

Steps 3, 4, 5, 6, 7 (back view)

7. Tuck the stem into the loop that was made when you bent the stem over the cord.

8. Slide the ti leaf close to other leaves you have put on the cord. Tighten the knot by pulling a little on the stem.

9. Trim the tips of the leaf stems so they are all about the same length and feel comfortable around your waist. Be careful not to cut the cord.

By tearing along the lines in each leaf you can give your skirt a fringed look. Tear from the midrib out to the edge of the leaf. Begin at the tip end of the leaf.

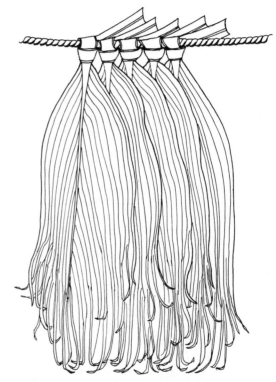

Steps 8, 9 (front view)

I. TI (KĪ OR LĀʻĪ)
6. *Ti Leaf Carrier, or Harness (ʻIli Kaʻa Lāʻī)*

Long ago people carried things down from the mountains. Sometimes they used a ti leaf harness, or carrier, to help them carry things on their backs. You can make a ti leaf carrier by following these directions.

WHAT YOU NEED

1. Thirty to forty large, green, deboned ti leaves. Directions for deboning ti leaves are in section I, 1. The actual number of ti leaves you need will depend on how large you make your carrier.
2. Two small ti leaves, green or brown.

WHAT TO DO

1. Take three large ti leaves of different lengths. Fold each leaf lengthwise into thirds with the shiny side showing.
2. Tie the tips of the three ti leaves together tightly with one of the small ti leaves.
3. Then braid the three ti leaves almost to their ends.
4. Add new folded ti leaves as the ends become short. To do this, just place a new folded leaf tip against the stem end of the first one and continue to braid very tightly. Add new leaves at different places in the braid. The tips of the

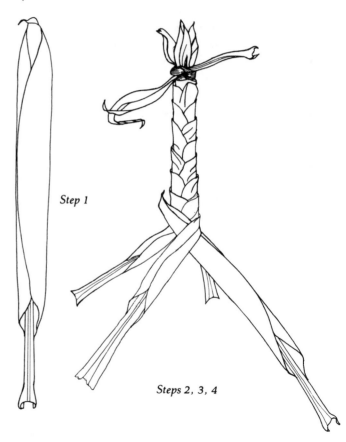

Step 1

Steps 2, 3, 4

newly added leaves can stick out. You can trim them later, if you like.

5. Continue braiding and adding ti leaves until your carrier is long enough. It needs to be long enough to go around the back of your neck, over your shoulders, under your armpits, cross over the bundle on your back that you are going to carry, and around to the front of your waist.

6. Use the second small ti leaf to tie the other end of the braid.

7. Knot the two ends of the long braid together at your waist. Or tie the ends of the two small ti leaves together at your waist.

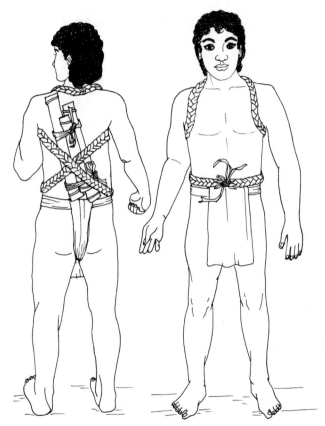

Steps 5, 6, 7

9

I. TI (KĪ OR LĀ'Ī)
7. Ti Leaf Sandals (Kāma'a Lā'ī)

Walking on lava and coral was hard on bare feet, so the Hawaiians made sandals to protect their feet. This is one way you can make ti leaf sandals.

WHAT YOU NEED

About twenty-five to thirty dried, deboned ti leaves for each sandal. You will need about fifty to sixty to make a pair of sandals. There are directions for deboning and drying ti leaves in sections I, 1 and I, 2.

WHAT TO DO

First make a long ti leaf braided rope:
1. Soak the ti leaves in water for about one hour. This will make them easier to handle.
2. Tear ten ti leaves in half for one sandal. Tear from the tip down through the stem.
3. Tie the stems of three half ti leaves of different lengths together.
4. Put the knot between your toes.
5. Braid the three half ti leaves tightly. Braid toward the tips. Stop braiding about six inches away from the tips. This is so you will have some unbraided inches for adding more leaves.

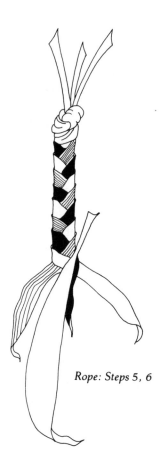

Rope: Steps 5, 6

6. To add more leaves put the stem end of another half ti leaf against the unbraided inches. Braid it into the first leaves tightly. Continue to add new half leaves and braid them into the braid. Add new leaves at different places in the braid. The tips and stems of newly added leaves can stick out. You can trim them later.
7. Continue braiding and adding ti leaves until the braid is six feet long.
8. End your braided rope with a knot.
9. Trim off any pieces that stick out.

Now that you have made the long braid, make the sandal padding. Use whole, dried, deboned ti leaves to make the padding, or the sole:
1. Tie the stems of two leaves together in a double knot.
2. Put these knotted leaves flat on the floor.
3. Next fold your ti leaf braid in half. Put the curved center of this braid on the floor just above the knot.
4. Bring the ti leaf on the right over the right side of the braid and under the left side of the braid. Bring the left ti leaf over the left side of the braid and under the right side of the braid. Leave about four inches of the braid showing in a curve above the sole.

Sole: Steps 1, 2, 3, 4

11

5. Continue doing this, weaving back and forth. Squeeze the ti leaves close together as you go. Push them up toward the curved center of the braid.

6. Add new ti leaves by placing the tip end of the new leaf against four inches of the old leaf. Then continue weaving as though the old leaf and new leaf were joined together.

7. Weave the leaves until the padding is the same size as your foot. Be sure the leaves are squeezed together tightly so you have a firm, padded sole.

8. Make a knot with the stems of the last two ti leaves to tie them together.

9. Divide the sole into thirds. Find a ti leaf stem at one end of the sole. Poke this stem into the padded sole about one-third of the way up. Tie it in a double knot to another stem near the first one in the sole.

10. Move up to the next third of the padded sole. Look for two more stems close to each other. Wrap them around the padding, each stem going around in the opposite direction so that they meet on the bottom. Tie them in double knots. Keep all the knots on one side. The side with the knots will be the bottom of the sandal.

11. Move up to the top third of the padded sole. Find two more stems. Wrap them around the padding, each stem

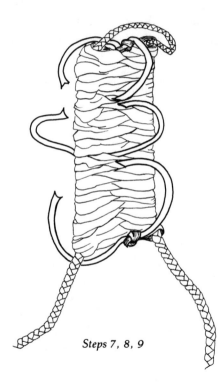

Steps 7, 8, 9

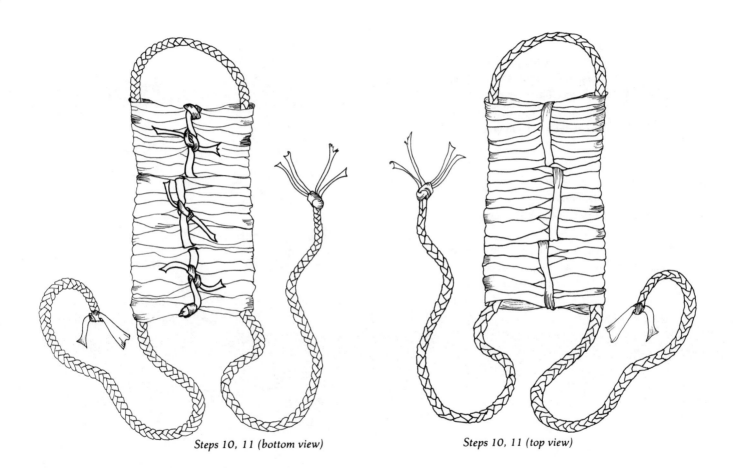

Steps 10, 11 (bottom view)   *Steps 10, 11 (top view)*   13

going around in the opposite direction so that they meet on the bottom. Tie them tightly. Remember that the side with the knots will be the bottom of the sandal.

Now you are ready to tie the sandal to your foot:

1. Put your foot on the padding.
2. Bring the curved braid, or toe loop, up over your toes. If the toe loop is too big, you can make it smaller by pulling on the ends of the braid.
3. Crisscross the open ends of the long braid behind your ankle.
4. Take one braid end and put it over, then under, the toe loop. Wrap this end around your ankle.
5. Wrap the other braid end around your ankle.
6. Tie the two braid ends at your ankle so that the sandal feels comfortable.

14

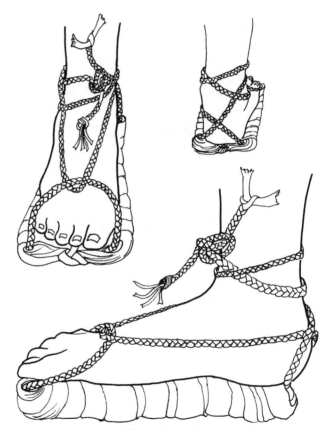

Tying the Sandal

II. COCONUT (NIU)

1. *How to Clean a Coconut Midrib (Nī'au)*

Hawaiians used coconut trees and their parts in many ways. You can find directions for using parts of the coconut in almost every section of this book. This section tells you a few of the ways.

WHAT YOU NEED

1. Some fresh coconut leaflets. Pull or cut them off a coconut frond.
2. Scissors or a sharp knife.

WHAT TO DO

1. Use your fingers to pull as much of the green leaflet away from the midrib as you can.
2. Hold the thick end of the midrib. Using the sharp edge of a scissors or a knife, scrape away the rest of the green part.
3. Trim off the bottom of the midrib neatly with the scissors.

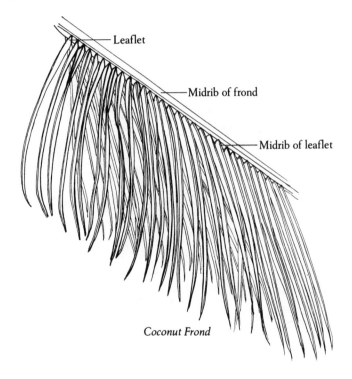

Leaflet

Midrib of frond

Midrib of leaflet

Coconut Frond

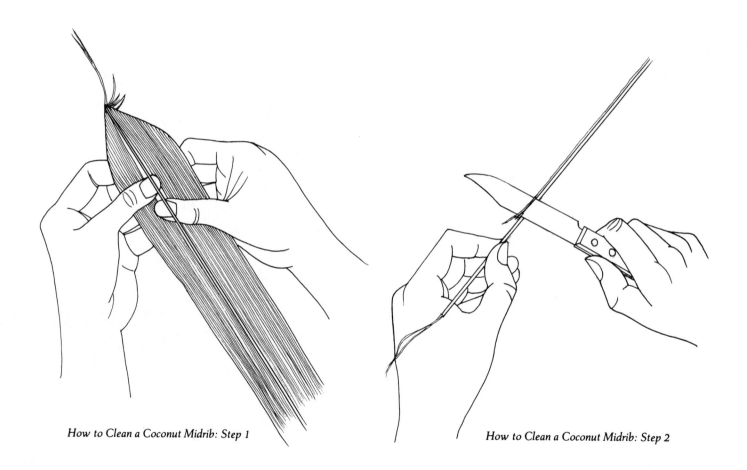

16   *How to Clean a Coconut Midrib: Step 1*   *How to Clean a Coconut Midrib: Step 2*

II. COCONUT (NIU)
2. *Coconut Midrib Lei Needle (Kui Nī'au)*

You can make a lei needle using a coconut midrib as the Hawaiians once did. Some people still use this kind of lei needle.

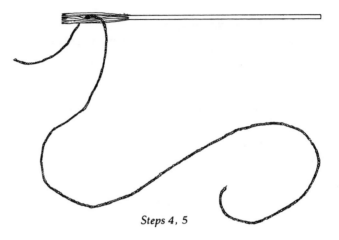

Steps 4, 5

WHAT YOU NEED

1. A cleaned coconut midrib. Section II, 1 tells you how to clean one.
2. A forty inch long string or thread for a neck lei.
3. Scissors.

WHAT TO DO

1. Cut the midrib so that you have about eight inches of the thickest part.
2. Trim the thick end of the midrib with the scissors so that it is neat.
3. Gently chew the thick end about an inch from the bottom to flatten and soften it.
4. Poke a small hole into this end. You could use the sharp point of the scissors. Sometimes the end of the midrib will become so soft that you can make an opening with your fingernail.
5. Pass one end of the string through the hole.

II. COCONUT (NIU)
3. *How to Make a Broom (Pūlumi Nī'au)*

The ancient Hawaiians used coconut midribs tied together with coconut cord to make brooms. You can easily make a broom.

WHAT YOU NEED

1. Eighty coconut leaflets. Use leaflets from the bottom of the fronds to make a stiffer broom.
2. Jute twine. Or you can make coconut fiber cord using the directions in section IV, 1.
3. Scissors.

WHAT TO DO

1. Clean the leaflets so that only the midribs are left. See section II, 1 for directions for doing this.
2. Gather the midribs by holding the thick ends together.
3. Tightly wind the twine around the thick ends a few times and knot it. Tightly wind another piece of twine around the midribs about four inches away from the first piece of twine and knot it.
4. Trim the thin ends so that each midrib is the same length.

Steps 2, 3, 4

18

II. COCONUT (NIU)
4. *How to Husk a Coconut #1 (Wehe I Ka Pulu Niu)*

The husk is the hard outer layer of the coconut. You need strong arms to husk a coconut. Hawaiians of long ago used a sharp stick. You can use a pickaxe instead of a stick.

Use the fibers in the husk to make cord, or sennit. Directions for doing this are in section IV, 1.

WHAT YOU NEED

1. A pickaxe.
2. A mature coconut.

WHAT TO DO

1. Sink the blunt end of the pickaxe into the ground. Make sure this end is in the ground firmly.
2. Pound the coconut husk about one-third of the way from the stem end on a hard surface. This will soften it a little.
3. Put one foot on the pickaxe handle. This will help to hold the pickaxe steady.
4. Hold the coconut at each end. Thrust or force the husk onto the point of the pickaxe. Do this where the husk was softened. Wiggle the husk to loosen it from the nut inside.
5. Pull and push the coconut so that the husk rips away from the nut inside. Pull or pry off a piece of husk.

6. Now turn the coconut a little. Thrust or force the husk onto the pickaxe point. Pull and push the coconut away from the pickaxe so a part of the husk rips away from the nut.
7. Keep doing this until the husk is completely removed.

If you have a hard time husking a coconut this way, try the next set of directions.

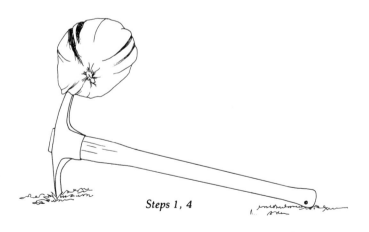

Steps 1, 4

19

II. COCONUT (NIU)
5. *How to Husk a Coconut #2 (Wehe I Ka Pulu Niu)*

WHAT YOU NEED

A mature coconut.

WHAT TO DO

1. Pound the end of the coconut opposite the stem end on a very hard surface. Pound until the husk softens and begins to split open about halfway up the coconut.
2. Then pound the stem end of the coconut on the hard surface. Pound until the other half of the husk splits open.
3. Pull the husk and inner fibers off the nut.

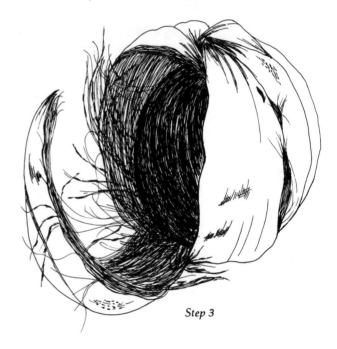

Step 3

III. TOOLS (NĀ PONO HANA)
1. *Kukui Nut Candle (Ihoiho Kukui)*

The Hawaiians burned kukui nuts for light. Many nuts were needed because each nut burned for only a short time.

   Make a kukui nut candle. See for yourself how long it takes for each nut to burn.

WHAT YOU NEED

1. Many husked kukui nuts.
2. A pan in which to roast the nuts.
3. A bucket of water.
4. A coconut midrib. Use the lower, stronger part of the midrib. You can find directions on how to clean the midrib in section II, 1. Or you can use a long, thin bamboo splinter or a barbecue stick.
5. Matches to light the candle.
6. A container filled with sand in which to stand the midrib or bamboo splinter.
7. A pan to put under the container to catch any burned nuts that might fall off.
8. A heavy-duty hammer.
9. A stick to knock off the burnt kukui nuts.

WHAT TO DO

1. Roast the nuts in an oven at 300° F. for about one hour.

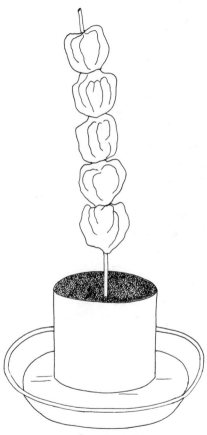

Steps 3, 4, 5

21

Then put them into a bucket of water for half an hour or so.

2. Hold the kukui nut on its side. Hit it lightly with the hammer. Try not to break the kernel inside.

3. Take out the kernel. Push the coconut midrib or bamboo splinter through the middle of each kernel. Make sure that each kernel is touching the one next to it.

4. Leave the lower part of the midrib or bamboo splinter empty.

5. Stick the coconut midrib or bamboo splinter into the sand-filled container. Put this container in the pan.

6. Light the top nut with a match.

7. Before the nut burns out, carefully take the midrib or bamboo splinter out of the sand-filled container. Turn the candle upside-down to light the next kernel. Use the stick to knock off the burnt kernel. Then put the candle back into the sand.

III. TOOLS (NĀ PONO HANA)
2. *Hawaiian Paint Brush (Hulu'ānai Hala)*

The hala tree has a round fruit. When this fruit falls from the tree, it breaks into sections, called keys, that are yellow or orange. When these sections are dried, they can be used as paint brushes.

WHAT YOU NEED

Sections, or keys, of hala fruit. Look under a hala tree. Sometimes you can find "brushes" there already dried. Or you can find a tree with fruit on it. Wait till the fruit ripens and falls.

WHAT TO DO

1. If the hala fruit keys are fresh (yellow or orange), put them in the sun to dry. Turn them over from time to time so both sides dry. This may take several weeks.
2. When the hala fruit keys are dry, or if you have found ones already dry, wash them in water so that the "brush" end is clean. Dry the brushes in the sun for several days. Turn them from time to time.
3. If you want narrow brushes, trim the dried keys to the size you want.
4. Now the brushes are ready to use for painting. You might want to paint with Hawaiian dye. There are directions for making dyes in section VIII.

Hala Fruit

Hawaiian Paint Brush

23

III. TOOLS (NĀ PONO HANA)
3. *Bamboo Stamp for Kapa ('Ohe Kāpala)*

Kapa, or tapa, is the cloth Hawaiians made from certain plants. Hawaiian *kapa* was the finest in all the Pacific. One of the tools used in decorating *kapa* was a stamp made of bamboo. A design was carved on each stamp. The stamp was dipped into a bowl of dye. The extra dye was removed by tapping the carved end gently against the rim of the bowl. Then the stamp was pressed onto the *kapa* several times to make a repeated design.

First prepare the bamboo.

WHAT YOU NEED

1. A stalk of bamboo.
2. A saw.
3. A hammer.
4. Sandpaper.
5. An X-acto knife with different kinds of blades.
6. A heavy knife.

WHAT TO DO

1. Use the saw to cut the bamboo at the ends of the internodes, or sections.
2. Stand the piece of cut bamboo upright. Place the sharp edge of a heavy knife on the top edge of the bamboo. Hit

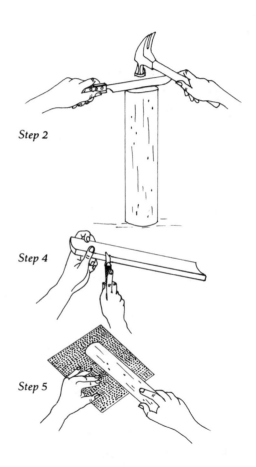

Step 2

Step 4

Step 5

24

the top of the knife with the hammer so that the bamboo splits in half.

3. Cut each half of this split bamboo into one- to one-and-a-half-inch strips using the knife and hammer.

4. Use the X-acto knife to scrape or cut away the curved, raised edges on the inner side of the bamboo. You want to make the printing surface as flat as possible.

5. Lay the sandpaper on a flat surface. Smooth the inner side of the bamboo by rubbing or pulling the bamboo across the sandpaper.

Make the bamboo stamp.

WHAT YOU NEED

1. A ruler.
2. A pencil.
3. An X-acto knife with different kinds of blades.
4. A triangle rasp, if you wish.

WHAT TO DO

1. Use the inner side of the bamboo for your design. Use the pencil and ruler to measure and mark off four one-inch sections on one end.

2. In each one-inch box draw your design. It is much easier

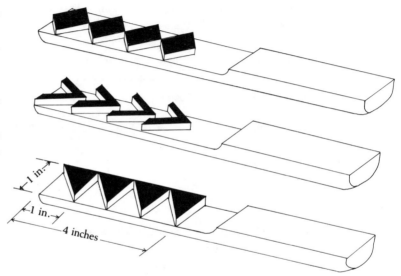

To Make the Bamboo Stamp: Steps 1, 2, 3

25

to make your first stamp design using straight lines in a simple pattern. Curved lines are harder to do.

3. Cut away the wood that is not part of your design. Use the X-acto knife and the triangle rasp to help you. Make sure that the parts you remove are cut cleanly and deeply so that you will have a neat print.

Now you can begin to print.

WHAT YOU NEED

1. Bamboo stamp(s).
2. Nonfusible pellon. You can buy the pellon in any fabric store.
3. Dyes in bowls. There are recipes for dyes in section VIII. Dyes that have been left in the sun to thicken for a day are best to use for printing. The introduction to the section on dyes will tell you more about this.
4. A paint brush or a hala paint brush. Directions for making a hala paint brush are in section III, 2.

WHAT TO DO

1. Dip the bamboo stamp into the bowl of dye. Gently tap it on the edge of the bowl to remove the extra dye. Press the stamp firmly onto the cloth. Repeat this until you have the pattern you want.

2. Another way to print is to dip the paint brush into the dye, paint the stamp, and then press the stamp onto the cloth. Make sure you do not brush too much dye onto the stamp or your pattern will look very messy.

You can also make designs on *kapa* by dipping a twisted cord into dye. Use dye that has been left in the sun to thicken for a day. Shake as much of the dye off the cord as you can. Have someone hold both ends of the cord very tightly just above your cloth. Snap the cord. This will make a pattern on your cloth. Some people think Hawaiians might have learned about this from watching ship carpenters make chalk lines with string.

Another way to make designs on *kapa* is to dip your Hawaiian paint brush into dye that has been left in the sun for a day to thicken. Paint directly onto the cloth.

III. TOOLS (NĀ PONO HANA)
4. Notes (Kekahi Mea Liʻiliʻi ʻĒ Aʻe)

Hawaiians of long ago found uses for many things. You can use some of the things they worked with to help you as you follow the directions in this book.

ʻOpihi shells can be used for peeling taro and grating coconuts. You can also use *ʻopihi* shells to scrape kukui nuts and other things that need to be cleaned or scraped.

Shells and sharks' teeth make good cutting tools. Thin pieces of bamboo can be used for cutting, too.

Pieces of bumpy coral can be used as a rough sandpaper.

The leaf sheath of the breadfruit tree dries and turns brown. You can often find some under a breadfruit tree. These can be used for polishing kukui nuts or used as a fine sandpaper.

The white sticky sap of the breadfruit tree can be used as glue.

The dried flower cluster of the coconut tree makes a good rake.

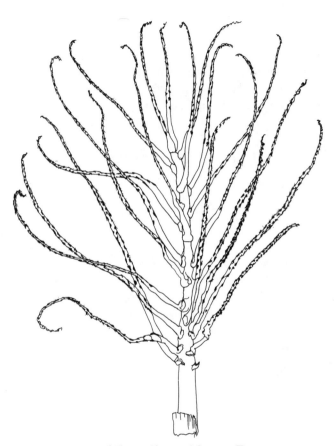

Dried Flower Cluster of Coconut Tree

27

IV. CORDAGE (AHO)

The Hawaiians of long ago did not have metal to make nails. They made cords to tie things together. They used cords in making canoes, tools, and many other things.

The pages in this section tell you how to prepare plant material to use for cordage. There are also pages that tell you some of the ways Hawaiians made cordage.

1. *Preparing Coconut Fiber, or Sennit, for Three-Ply Cord ('Aha Ka'ā Kolu)*

WHAT YOU NEED

Large, mature coconuts.

WHAT TO DO

1. Pull the husk from a coconut into eight or ten sections. There are directions for husking a coconut in section II, 4 and II, 5.
2. Soak the coconut husk sections in water for several days.
3. Pound the outside of the coconut husk pieces. This will loosen the fibers a little.
4. Pull the inside fibers from the husk. Twist and wiggle them away from the husk without breaking the fibers.
5. Clean the fibers by running your thumbnail over them.
6. Put three fibers together on your thigh. Roll them down to your knee. Do this several times. Pressing down firmly as you roll will make the fibers twist together. Put a little coconut oil on your thigh to make this easier.
7. When you have several twists of fiber ready, braid them together. A three-strand braid is easiest to make.

Step 4

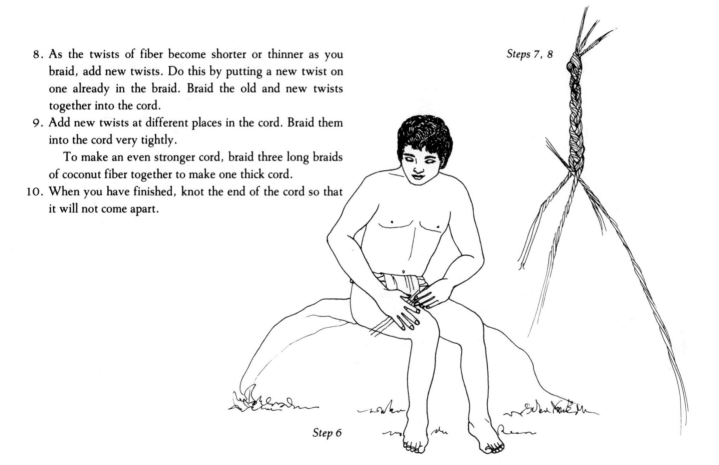

8. As the twists of fiber become shorter or thinner as you braid, add new twists. Do this by putting a new twist on one already in the braid. Braid the old and new twists together into the cord.

9. Add new twists at different places in the cord. Braid them into the cord very tightly.

   To make an even stronger cord, braid three long braids of coconut fiber together to make one thick cord.

10. When you have finished, knot the end of the cord so that it will not come apart.

Steps 7, 8

Step 6

29

IV. CORDAGE (AHO)

2. *Preparing Hau Fiber for Cord (Aho Hau)*

Hau trees grow near many beaches. You can use the inner fiber of hau branches to make cords. These directions tell you one of several ways to get strips of inner fiber from branches of the hau tree.

WHAT YOU NEED

1. A hau branch.
2. A saw.
3. A sharp knife.
4. A dull knife.
5. A bucket.

WHAT TO DO

1. Find a young branch that is about three inches around and a yard or more long on a hau tree. Look for one that does not have many smaller branches growing from it.
2. Saw the branch from the tree.
3. Use a sharp knife to lift a piece of the dark, outer bark together with its inner layers away from the rest of the branch. This piece should be a half inch to one inch wide. Begin lifting this piece at the sawed end of the branch.
4. Pull this piece away from the branch. Strip it straight down from the sawed end toward the tip.

30

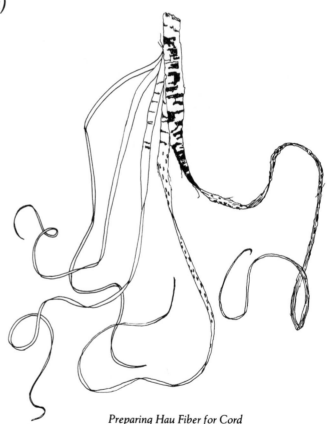

Preparing Hau Fiber for Cord

5. Pull as many strips away from the branch as you can. These strips can be different lengths.

6. Put the strips into a bucket of water. Be sure the water covers all of them.

7. After a few days, use a dull knife to scrape or peel away the dark, outer bark from the strips. Do this so that water can get into the inner layers more easily.

8. Soak the inner layers about two or three weeks. Change the water often to keep it from becoming smelly.

9. Rub the inner layers between your fingers to help separate them. Pull the layers apart.

10. Pull each layer across the blade of a dull knife several times. This will clean them and remove the sap.

11. Dry the strips in a shady place.

You can use the strips of hau inner layers to make cords by following the directions in sections IV, 1; IV, 4; and IV, 5.

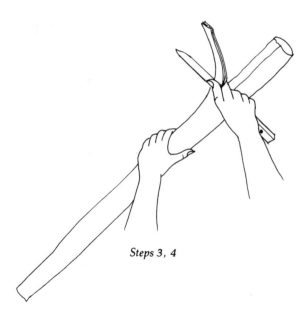

Steps 3, 4

IV. CORDAGE (AHO)
3. *Preparing Ti Leaves for Cord (Aho Lā'ī)*

You can use dried, deboned ti leaves for making cords. There are directions for deboning ti leaves and for drying them in sections I, 1 and I, 2. Dried ti leaves that you find on plants or on the ground can be used for cord, too. Soak them in water for about an hour. This will make them soft enough to use in making cord.

4. *Two-Ply Cord (Aho Ka'ā Lua)*

The directions below use ti leaves to make cord. You can use hau fiber or raffia to make cords in this way, too.

WHAT YOU NEED

Dried, deboned ti leaves that have been soaked in water for an hour.

WHAT TO DO

1. Tear the brown ti leaves in half. Tear from the tip down to the stem.
2. Put a half leaf around the back of a toe. Bring the tip end and stem end toward you.

3. Tightly twist about an inch of the right half of the leaf to the left.
4. Tightly twist about an inch of the left half to the left.
5. Now keeping the tight twists in the two halves, wind them around each other by winding to the right several times.
6. Continue to twist the two halves of the cord to the left and then wind them together to the right.
7. To add more leaves, put a half ti leaf on a leaf that is being twisted. Twist the added leaf with the old one. Then wind the added leaf into the cord. The ends of newly added leaves will stick out, but you can trim them later.
8. Knot the end of the cord when it is finished so it will not come apart.

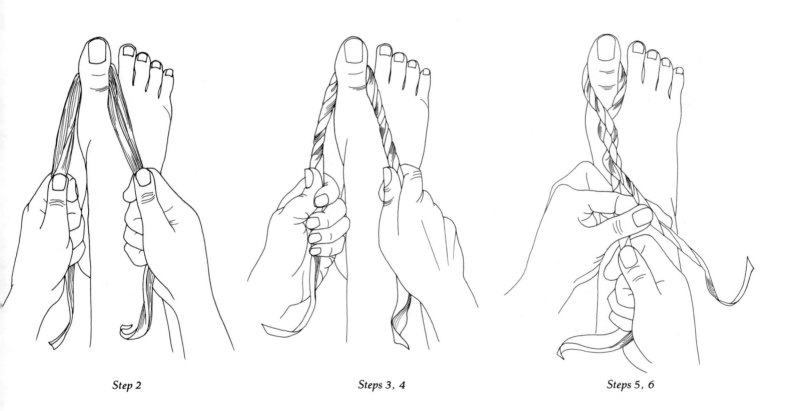

Step 2   Steps 3, 4   Steps 5, 6

33

IV. CORDAGE (AHO)
5. *Five-Ply Cord (Aho Kaʻā Lima)*

Use hau fiber to follow these directions for making a five-ply braid. Directions for preparing hau fiber for cords are in section IV, 2. If you do not have hau, you could use raffia.

WHAT YOU NEED
Five strips of hau fiber about thirty inches long.

WHAT TO DO

1. Put the five strips of hau together. Make a loop at one end and knot it. Slip the loop over your big toe.
2. Pull the five strips toward you. Make them flat.
3. Pick up the strip on the outside right. Bring it over and across the next two middle strips. Pull tightly.
4. Next pick up the strip on the outside left. Bring it over and across the two strips next to it. Pull tightly.
5. Continue to bring the right outside strip over and across two strips, and the left outside strip over and across two strips. Make sure you pull tightly after each crossing.
6. When you have finished, tie the ends in a knot so the strips will not come apart.

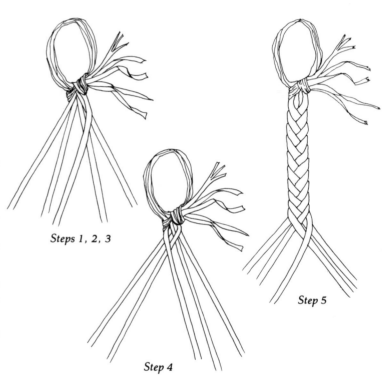

Steps 1, 2, 3

Step 4

Step 5

V. TOYS (NĀ MEA PĀʻANI)
1. *Spinning Top (Hū)*

Some people say the *menehune* used kukui nuts for tops. You can make spinning tops out of kukui nuts by following these directions.

WHAT YOU NEED

1. A kukui nut that has a pointed nose, or tip. You may have to peel away the soft outer layer to get to the nut.
2. Some very thin splinters of bamboo about the size of a toothpick. You can use a toothpick if you do not have bamboo.
3. A rat-tail file.

WHAT TO DO

1. Scrape or sand away any outer covering that may be left on the kukui nut you use. You could scrape the nut with an *ʻopihi* shell.
2. At the stem end of the nut, the end opposite the pointed tip, file on the ridge to make a groove. File until you begin to see a little spot of the nutmeat inside the nut. You will be able to do this in a short time. The spot of meat needs to be only about as big as the tip of your bamboo or toothpick.

3. The place where the nutmeat shows through will be soft. Push a thin splinter of bamboo or a toothpick into this place to finish your top.
4. Twirl your top between your thumb and fingers to make it spin.

Steps 2, 3

V. TOYS (NĀ MEA PĀʻANI)
2. *String Figure (Hei)*

Hawaiians enjoyed making string figures, or *hei*. Many of these *hei* were made while chanting. Here are directions for a simple one-eyed figure. It is a fish. It has a chant to go with it.

WHAT YOU NEED

A piece of string, five or six feet long.

WHAT TO DO

1. Knot the two ends of the string together.
2. Place the string around your left thumb and your left little finger, crossing your palm. Let the rest of the string hang down.
3. Pass your right thumb from right to left through the lower loop of the hanging string. Turn your thumb toward your body to twist the string and then hold your thumb upright.
4. Your right little finger goes under the right thumb string closest to it, then stands upright. You should have a figure X.
5. Your right index finger goes under the string on your left hand that crosses the palm. Your left index finger goes under the string at the base of the right index finger. Pull both hands apart and hold your fingers upright.

6. Drop the string from both thumbs. Pass your thumbs over the top of the strings and under the second to the last string on your little fingers. Hold your fingers upright.
7. Swing both hands up and down as you say this chant:

Pūlehu ka nenue.	Roasted, the *nenue.*
Kōʻala ka nenue.	Broiled, the *nenue.*

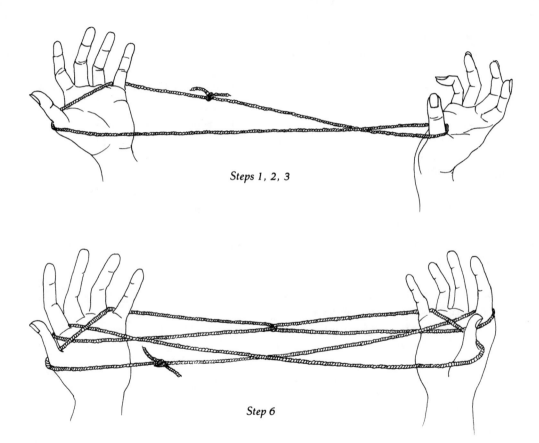

Steps 1, 2, 3

Step 6

V. TOYS (NĀ MEA PĀ'ANI)
3. *Kamani Nut Whistle (Oeoe Kamani)*

The true kamani tree has a round nut. By following these directions, you can make a whistle from kamani nuts you find under a tree.

WHAT YOU NEED

1. A mature true kamani nut.
2. A strong knife with a sharp point.
3. A paper clip to clean out the inside of the nut.
4. A piece of cord or string about six feet long.

WHAT TO DO

1. Peel or scrape off the wrinkled outside of the nut.
2. Using the sharp point of a knife, poke a hole at the top, or stem end, of the nut. Make this hole about one-half inch wide.
3. Clean out the meat inside the nut. Do not eat any of this meat because it can make you sick. Clean out the meat by poking a paper clip into the nut and digging out the meat.
4. Make a smaller hole about a quarter of an inch to the right of the big hole.
5. Make another small hole about a quarter of an inch to the left of the big hole.
6. Thread the cord or string into the small holes. Put the thread into the small hole on the right side. Go under the big hole and bring the thread out through the small hole on the left.
7. Slip the whistle to the middle of the cord. Then tie the ends of the cord together.
8. Swing the whistle in the air as fast as you can. The air rushing through the larger hole will make a soft whistling sound.

You can also make a whistle by putting only one hole in the top or stem end of the kamani nut. Clean it out very well and wash it to be sure all the meat is cleaned off. Blowing into this hole the way people blow into bottles will make a whistling sound.

Steps 4, 5, 6, 7

V. TOYS (NĀ MEA PĀʻANI)
4. *Ti Leaf Whistle (Pū Lāʻī)*

WHAT YOU NEED

1. One fresh, green ti leaf.
2. One small, thin splinter of bamboo about the size of a toothpick. You can use a toothpick if you don't have any bamboo.

WHAT TO DO

1. Take the bone, or midrib, out of the ti leaf. You can find directions for doing this in section I, 1.
2. Tear the leaf in half starting at the pointed tip of the leaf.
3. Cut off the stem.
4. Beginning at the tip, roll the half leaf keeping it very tight.
5. Fasten this roll together with a splinter of bamboo or a toothpick.
6. Press the roll with your fingers so that it changes from a round shape to an oval shape.
7. Blow hard. You can squeeze the leaf to get a sound. Do not squeeze so hard that air cannot get through. Try squeezing your whistle in different places to get different sounds.

Step 4

Steps 5, 6

39

V. TOYS (NĀ MEA PĀ'ANI)
5. *Bent Coconut Midrib (Panapana Nī'au)*

Even little children can enjoy playing with this toy that was made by Hawaiian children long ago.

WHAT YOU NEED

1. At least one fresh coconut midrib per player. You can find directions for cleaning midribs in section II, 1.
2. Scissors.

WHAT TO DO

1. Trim the midrib to the size you can bend easily with one hand.
2. Bend the midrib into a curve. Hold it tightly between your thumb and middle finger. Bend the midrib away from your hand.
3. Let go quickly so that the midrib springs away from you.
4. You can make this into a contest by aiming at a target to see who comes closest. Or you can see who can spring the midrib the farthest.

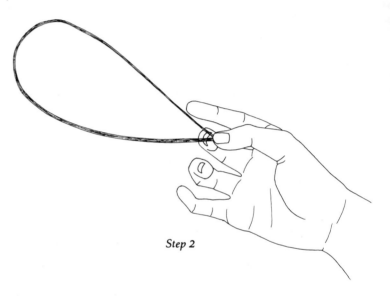

Step 2

V. TOYS (NĀ MEA PĀʻANI)
6. *Loop and Ball Game (Palaʻie)*

Early Hawaiians made toys from parts of the coconut. You can make a toy called *palaʻie* to play a loop and ball game of the same name by following these directions.

WHAT YOU NEED

1. Twelve or fifteen stripped coconut midribs twenty-eight inches or longer. Fresh ones are easier to braid and bend. Look at section II, 1 to find out how to strip coconut midribs.
2. Two pieces of twine that are ten inches long and one piece of twine that is thirty-six inches long.
3. Small pieces of cloth-like coconut fiber from the base of the coconut fronds to lightly crumple into a ball and one piece of coconut fiber about nine inches square. You will use this larger piece to wrap around the smaller pieces.
4. A long needle with an eye large enough to thread the twine.

WHAT TO DO

Make the coconut midrib loop:

1. Trim the bottom ends of the midribs so that they are even and neat.
2. Hold these ends together tightly. Wind a ten-inch piece of

Loop: Steps 1, 2, 3, 4, 5

41

twine tightly around the ends several times. Tie it in a tight square knot. Trim the ends, leaving about two inches of twine.

3. Divide the midribs into three equal bundles. Then braid them tightly beginning at the tied end. Braid as far down to the tips of the midribs as you can. Keep the midribs flat as you braid.

4. Gently bend the tips of the braided midribs to form a loop that will hold the weight of the ball. You can see what this will look like in the picture of the finished *pala'ie* stick.

5. Use the other ten-inch piece of twine to fasten the loop to the handle. Wind it around tightly several times and make a tight square knot. Trim the tips of the midribs so that they are neat. Do not trim them too close to the knot.

Make the ball:

1. Loosely crumple some small pieces of coconut fiber into a ball in your hand.

2. Wrap this ball with the nine-inch square of coconut fiber. Make sure your ball is lightweight and only a little larger than the loop of the *pala'ie*.

3. Tightly wind one end of the thirty-six inch piece of twine

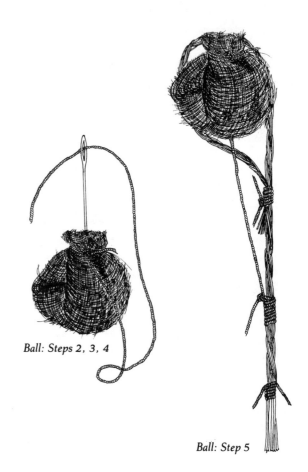

Ball: Steps 2, 3, 4

Ball: Step 5

several times around the top of the coconut fiber wrapping. Then tie the twine in a tight square knot.

4. Thread the other end of this piece of twine with the needle. Pass the threaded needle through the center of the tied part of the ball, into the ball, and out the opposite end.

5. Slip the needle off the twine and tie that end of the twine to the middle of the *pala'ie* handle. The twine should be just long enough for the ball to sit in the center of the loop. Tie it to the handle so that this knot is directly below the loop. Trim any extra twine from the ball and from the handle.

Now you can use the *pala'ie:*

1. If you are right-handed, hold your *pala'ie* stick in your right hand with the loop on the left side of the handle.

2. Now swing your arm up and down. This will make the ball move in a circle over and under the loop. Try to get the ball to land in the loop as you swing it under and as you swing it over.

VI. GAMES (NĀ PĀʻANI)

1. Hawaiian Checkers (Kōnane)

In old Hawaiʻi *kōnane* boards were made on large flat stones or made from pieces of wood. The boards were of many different sizes. King Kamehameha I was very good at playing *kōnane*. You can learn to play it by following these directions.

WHAT YOU NEED

1. A *kōnane* board.
2. Thirty-two black pebbles. Or you can use thirty-two small pieces of black lava.
3. Thirty-two white pebbles. Or you can use thirty-two small pieces of white coral.

You can buy a set for playing *kōnane* in several stores in Hawaiʻi. You can make your own board at the beach by drawing the outline of a square in the sand. Find a flat place where the sand is hard. The square should be twelve by twelve inches. Make sixty-four marks in the square with your finger. You do this by making eight straight rows of eight marks across. You need to find thirty-two black pebbles and thirty-two white pebbles.

HOW TO GET READY

1. Fill all the holes or marks on the board with pebbles.

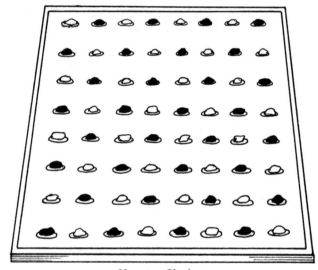

Hawaiian Checkers

Every other one should be black. Put the white pebbles on the board between the black ones.

2. Two players sit facing each other across the board. One player picks up one black pebble and one white pebble from the middle of the board. He puts the two pebbles behind his back and mixes them up in his hands. Then he shows his fists to the other player so that that player cannot see which pebble is in which hand. The second player touches one of the fists. The color of the pebble in that fist will be his color. The player that gets the black pebble will go first. Put those two pebbles beside the board.

HOW TO PLAY

1. The player using black stones moves a black stone over a white stone to an empty space. He takes the white stone he jumped over off the board and keeps it beside him.

2. The player using the white stones moves a white stone over a black stone to an empty space and keeps the black stone beside him.

3. Each time a player moves he must jump over one of the other player's stones. Players may jump over more than one stone. Each jump must be over only one stone at a time to an empty space. A player may jump forward or backward (toward the other player or away from him) or left or right. He may not move diagonally. And he may not move in two directions in one turn.

4. The game is over when a player is unable to move.

HOW TO SCORE

1. The winner of the game is the player who makes the last move on the board. This means that you will want to be sure you still have stones you can move near the end of the game. You want to make the other player move his stones so that he cannot move by the end of the game.

2. You may also decide that the winner will be the one who has the most stones. You should decide how to win before you start to play.

VI. GAMES (NĀ PĀ'ANI)
2. *Finding a Pebble under a Cloth (No'a)*

Both children and adults played this game in old Hawai'i. Good players learn to watch faces and motions very carefully.

WHAT YOU NEED

1. A *no'a*, or stone, about the size of a quarter.
2. A *maile*, or stick, to use for pointing. You can tie a piece of *kapa* or a piece of ti leaf to the end of a stick. This will make it look like the pointing stick the Hawaiians used.
3. Pieces of *kapa* or cloth the size of a large handkerchief. If ten people are going to play, you will need five pieces of cloth. You need the same number of pieces of cloth as there are players on one team.

HOW TO PLAY

1. Form two teams. The people on one team sit across from the people on the other team, facing each other, about three feet apart.
2. Put the five pieces of cloth on the floor between the two teams.
3. The person to hide the stone holds it in her hand so that no one can see it. Then she lifts the edge of one of the pieces of cloth and puts her hand under it. She does this with each piece of cloth. She drops the stone under one of the pieces of cloth, but she tries hard not to let the people on the other team know which cloth has the stone under it.
4. The team that is watching will guess which cloth has the stone under it. When the members of that team have decided which cloth the stone is under, they point to that cloth with the pointing stick.
5. The watching team watches very carefully. That team might look at the face of the person who is hiding the stone, or watch her arm, or watch for other clues that might tell where the stone is. The person who is hiding the stone tries to fool the other team and not let those players know where the stone is.
6. Each team takes turns hiding the stone until one team has found it ten times.

HOW TO SCORE

1. Every time a team guesses where the stone is, that team gets a point. The first team to get ten points wins.
2. Another way to win is to get a point every time a team points to a cloth without the stone under it. The first team to get ten points wins the game.

You can play this game on the beach using piles of sand instead of pieces of cloth. You may find a shell or a piece of coral to use in place of a stone.

Finding a Pebble under a Cloth

47

VI. GAMES (NĀ PĀ'ANI)
3. *Finding a Pebble (Pūhenehene)*

This game is a little like the game called *no'a*, but in old Hawai'i it was played indoors and there was a different way of hiding the stone.

WHAT YOU NEED

1. A large piece of *kapa* or a cloth that is big enough to cover all the members of a team. You could use a blanket or a tablecloth.
2. A *no'a*, or stone, about the size of a quarter.

HOW TO PLAY

1. Form two teams. The people on one team sit across from the people on the other team, facing each other, about three feet apart.
2. The large piece of cloth is put over the members of one team so that they are hiding under it.
3. The people under the cloth hide the stone on one of their players. It could be in a sleeve, under a belt, or in one of the player's pockets. When the team is ready to play, they say *pūheoheo* to tell the other team that they are ready.
4. They take the large cloth away and sit facing the other team. They can put their heads down so the other team will not see their faces. This will make it harder for the other team to guess where the stone is.
5. Now the other team guesses which person has the stone. They look at the players for clues to help them guess correctly.

HOW TO SCORE

When the guessing team guesses correctly which person has the stone, it gets one point. If it guesses the wrong person, the team that hid the stone gets a point. The first team to get ten points wins.

Finding a Pebble

VI. GAMES (NĀ PĀʻANI)
4. Picking up Stones (Kimo)

Children, adults, and even high chiefs played this game in ancient Hawaiʻi. It is a little like jacks. *Kimo* means ''to bob.'' Sometimes it is called the head-bobbing game because people's heads bob up and down when they play it.

WHAT YOU NEED

Fifty or more pebbles or stones. You can find small pebbles on beaches and in streams. Or you can use the sections, or keys, from the hala tree fruit instead of pebbles.

HOW TO PLAY

1. Two players sit facing each other.
2. They place a pile of small stones or pebbles between them.
3. Each player picks out one stone for his own. This is called the *kimo* stone. He uses this whenever it is his turn.
4. A player always uses only one hand. He can use either his left hand or his right hand. He can not use both hands.
5. With one hand, he tosses his *kimo* stone up into the air. Using that same hand, he quickly picks up one stone before the *kimo* stone he tossed comes down. Then using that same hand, he catches his *kimo* stone as it comes down. He puts the stones he picked up beside him. He

does this until he misses. Then it is the other player's turn. They take turns until all the stones are picked up.

HOW TO SCORE

Players keep all the stones they pick up at their sides. When all the stones are picked up, they count the stones they have. The one with the most stones is the winner.

Picking up Stones

51

VI. GAMES (NĀ PĀʻANI)
5. *Sliding Coconut Shells (Kilu)*

In ancient Hawaiʻi *kilu* was played by chiefs and chiefesses. It was played in a thatched house that was built especially for playing this game. You can play it best by having the players sit on a smooth floor.

WHAT YOU NEED

1. A half coconut shell cut lengthwise to be the *kilu*.
2. Half coconut shells cut crosswise or small pieces of wood for each player.

HOW TO PLAY

1. Divide the players into two teams.
2. If there are many players, one person on each team can be the scorekeeper for her team.
3. One team sits facing the other team about ten to fifteen feet away.
4. One team places a coconut shell cut crosswise, open side down, in front of each player on the team.
5. A member of the other team puts a half coconut shell cut lengthwise, open side down, in front of her. She slides this shell toward the other team, aiming at a coconut shell in front of one of the players.
6. The players take turns until all the players on one team have had a turn. Then the other team takes its turn.

HOW TO SCORE

Every time one of the shells is hit, the team that slid the *kilu* gets one point. The team that gets ten points first is the winner.

Sliding Coconut Shells

53

VI. GAMES (NĀ PĀʻANI)
6. *Pulling Hooked Fingers (Loulou)*

Hawaiians of long ago played this game to develop strong hand and finger muscles.

WHAT YOU NEED

1. Pairs of players.
2. A referee for each pair.

HOW TO PLAY

1. The referee calls, ''Get ready!''
2. Each player steps up to her partner. The right little toe of one player's foot is placed next to her partner's right little toe. During the game the left foot may move, but the right foot must stay in this position.
3. Each player holds out her right hand with the index finger straight out. Her thumb should be flat on the palm. Her other three fingers hold down the thumb.
4. Her index finger is then curved around the other player's like a hook.
5. Players could also use other fingers of their right hands. They must be sure that the rest of the fingers are flat against the palm of the hand.
6. The referee calls, ''Begin!''

7. Each player pulls her hooked finger back slowly. Players are not allowed to jerk suddenly.

HOW TO SCORE

1. The one who can make the other player's finger straighten wins a point.
2. If a player moves her right foot out of position, she loses.
3. This game can also be played so that the winner is the person who first makes ten points.

Pulling Hooked Fingers

VI. GAMES (NĀ PĀʻANI)
7. Chest Pushing (Kulaʻi Umauma)

This game was played in old Hawaiʻi to use arm and leg muscles and to develop balance. The goal of this game is to push the other player off balance.

WHAT YOU NEED

1. Players in pairs.
2. A referee for each pair.

HOW TO PLAY

1. The referee calls, ''Get ready!''
2. The two players step up and face each other. Their arms are held out, hands up, and fingers together.
3. The referee calls, ''Begin!''
4. Each player steps forward and pushes or slaps the other's chest with his flat palms.

HOW TO SCORE

1. A player can win a point by making the other player fall down. He can also win a point by pushing the other player back out of position.
2. Another way to play this game is to stand facing each other with the little toes of the right feet touching. A point is won by pushing or slapping the other player's chest so that his right foot moves out of position.
3. The first player to push over the other player three times is the winner.

VI. GAMES (NĀ PĀʻANI)
8. *Foot Pushing (Kulaʻi Wāwae)*

This old Hawaiian game tests the strength of your leg muscles.

WHAT YOU NEED

1. Pairs of players.
2. A referee for each pair.

HOW TO PLAY

1. Each player sits facing his partner. They sit far enough apart so that their knees are slightly bent. The toes and balls of their feet should touch each other.
2. Their hands should be flat behind them. Their arms should be straight. This will hold their bodies in position.
3. The referee calls, ''Get ready!''
4. The referee calls, ''Begin!''
5. Each player pushes his feet against the other player's feet. A player can push straight ahead so that the other player is moved backwards. Or he can try to push the other player's feet to the right or left side.

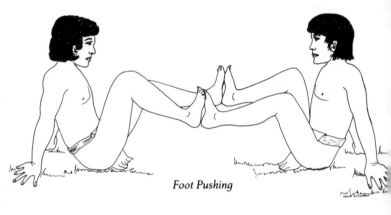

Foot Pushing

HOW TO SCORE

A player wins if he moves his partner away from him or out of his sitting position.

VII. LEIS AND LEI CARRIERS (NĀ LEI A ME NĀ MEA LAWE I LEI)

There were many kinds of leis in old Hawai'i. There were special leis for dancing the hula. Other leis were given as gifts.

Leis were made of flowers, leaves, vines, ferns, berries, and even seaweed. Leis were made of shells, animal teeth, and seeds, too.

Lei contests are held on Lei Day, May first, on all the Hawaiian islands. Lei contests are good places to learn how to make leis. The directions on the next pages in this book will help you learn how to make a few of the many kinds of leis.

1. *Lei Kui*

This is a way of making leis by stringing flowers through their centers or sides. You can string flowers, flower buds, berries, and many other things.

The directions below tell you how to string plumeria blossoms to make an easy lei.

WHAT YOU NEED

1. A strong thread about forty inches long.
2. A needle. You could use a needle made from the midrib of

Steps 3, 4

a coconut leaflet. There are directions for making one in section II, 2.

3. About thirty-six plumeria blossoms.

WHAT TO DO

1. Thread the needle.
2. Hold the stem end of the flower.
3. Push the needle into the center of the flower and out the stem end.
4. Pull the flower carefully toward the end of the thread, but do not pull it all the way to the end. Leave about three inches of the thread empty so you will be able to tie it easily.
5. Continue adding flowers until there are about three inches left at the end of the thread.
6. Slip the needle off the thread. Tie the ends of the thread in a square knot.

VII. LEIS AND LEI CARRIERS (NĀ LEI A ME NĀ MEA LAWE I LEI)
2. *Lei Kuipapa*

This is a way of sewing a lei to a flat backing. The backing may be a folded ti leaf, banana bark, hala leaf, hau fiber, or even a strip of cloth. The flowers or ferns are sewed to a backing with needle and thread. This lei is often used as a hat lei.

WHAT YOU NEED

1. One large, fresh green ti leaf. It should fit around your hat with about two inches to spare.
2. Needle and thread. Use a single thread when you sew. Knot the bottom end of the thread.
3. You can use almost any kind of flowers and leaves. Plan the pattern you want to have. Also decide whether you want your lei to look full or dainty.

WHAT TO DO

1. Trim the stems of your flowers and put them in water for at least an hour before you begin to make your lei.
2. Debone the ti leaf. Directions for doing this are in section I, 1. Fold the ti leaf in thirds lengthwise with the shiny side showing.
3. Decide on a pattern of flowers and leaves.
4. Place a row of plant material across the width of the ti

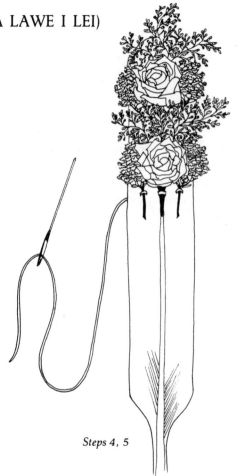

Steps 4, 5

59

leaf. Hold this in place by stitching one or two times over each stem.

5. Place your second row of plant material over the first row. Make it overlap the first row and hide the stitching. Stitch each stem in the second row to the backing.

6. Continue to add to your lei in this way.

7. When your lei is long enough to go around your hat with about two inches to spare, put the beginning part of the lei over the other end. Stitch the two ends together and knot the thread to hold the lei in place. Trim the extra leaf and thread.

VII. LEIS AND LEI CARRIERS (NĀ LEI A ME NĀ MEA LAWE I LEI)
3. *Lei Hili*

This is a way of making leis by braiding just one kind of material. Often fern leis are made this way.

Sometimes hula dancers wear *lei hili* made of ferns on their heads. The directions below tell you how to make a fern lei to wear on your head.

WHAT YOU NEED

About twenty or twenty-five fronds, or leaves, of *palapalai* or *pala'ā* fern. Each of the fronds should be about ten or twelve inches long.

The roots of ferns are not very deep. Be careful when you pick fern fronds not to pull up any roots. Pick them from several different spots. Pick only as much as you need.

WHAT TO DO

1. Hold three fronds of different lengths together.
2. Braid them from the middle of the fronds down toward the firm stem ends.
3. When there are only about three inches of the stems left to braid, add new fern. To do this, push a new firm stem end into the section you have braided. The lacy tip of this new fern frond should point in the opposite direction of the first three tips. Braid the added fern tightly into the stems of the first three ferns.

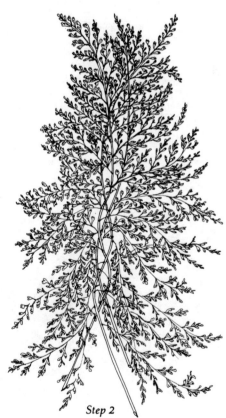

Step 2

61

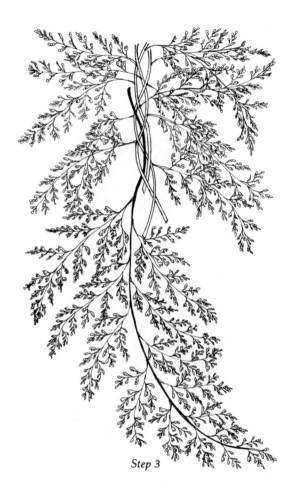

Step 3

4. Add another fern frond by again pushing a firm stem end into the braided section. The lacy tip of this new frond should point in the opposite direction of the first three tips. Braid it into the stems of the first three fern fronds.
5. Add a third new fern frond in the same way. As you add new fronds, be sure the firm stem ends are pushed through the braid to the same side.
6. Continue to add new fronds until the lei will go around your head and there are about eight extra inches.
7. Carefully trim the stem ends that are poking through the back of the lei so that the lei will feel comfortable around your head.
8. Wrap the lei around your head. To close the lei, twist the extra inches around each other at the back of your head.

Palapalai and *pala'ā* ferns can be kept green and fresh for a long time. Wrap them in wet paper towels and keep them in a tightly closed plastic bag, in a cool place. This is a good way to freshen a fern lei, too.

Save your lei until it is dry and brown. Use the dried *pala'ā* ferns to make dye. Directions for making dye using dried ferns are in section VIII, 9.

VII. LEIS AND LEI CARRIERS (NĀ LEI A ME NĀ MEA LAWE I LEI)
4. *Lei Haku*

This is a way of making a lei by braiding more than one kind of material. Long-stemmed flowers, leaves, and even fruits are braided with ferns, ti leaves, or the dried inner layers of banana or hau.

The directions that follow will help you make a head lei using ferns and long-stemmed flowers.

WHAT YOU NEED

1. At least twenty fresh fronds, or leaves, of *palapalai* or *palaʻā* fern. The number you use depends on the length of your lei. Each frond should be about ten to twelve inches long.

   When your lei is finished it should be about two to three inches bigger than your head size.

   The roots of ferns are not very deep. Be careful not to pull up any roots. Pick only as much fern as you need.

2. Flowers with stems two to three inches long. The number you use will depend on their size and the length of your lei. Some easy flowers to use are roses, daisies, chrysanthemums, and statice.

3. An eight-inch piece of string to tie your lei.

WHAT TO DO

1. Before you begin to braid, plan the pattern of your lei. You need to decide where to add flowers as you braid.

   You must also decide what colors you will use in your lei. The flowers you use will depend upon whether you want your lei to have few or many colors. It depends, too, upon whether you want your lei to look dainty or full.

2. Hold three fronds of different lengths together. Start to braid them about two or three inches from the top of the fronds. Braid these fronds together at least twice before you add flowers.

3. Put a flower in the center of the fronds. Then braid the two outside fronds over it to lock it in place. You may add another flower at this point. Or you may braid the fronds a few more times and then add another flower.

4. Add another fern frond when you have about three inches of stem left. To do this, put a new frond tip into the section you have already braided. Lay it right on top of the short stem end. Begin to braid this new frond two or three inches from its tip along with the first short stem end. Braid it tightly into the other stems as you add more flowers.

63

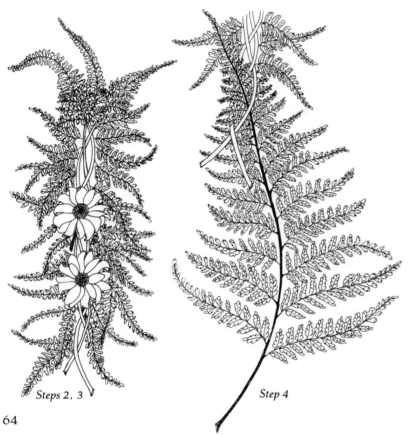

Steps 2, 3

Step 4

5. Continue to add ferns and flowers in the pattern you planned.

6. When your lei goes around your head with two to three inches to spare, you are ready to end it. Put the stem end of the lei under the tip end. Wind the string around the ends tightly and knot it. Try to wind the string so that it is hidden under the fern leaflets. Trim the string ends.

Keep your lei fresh by wrapping it in damp paper towels or newspaper. Store it in a tightly closed plastic bag in the refrigerator.

When your lei is dry and brown, use the dried *pala'ā* ferns to make dye. Directions for this are in section VIII, 9.

VII. LEIS AND LEI CARRIERS (NĀ LEI A ME NĀ MEA LAWE I LEI)
5. *Lei Wili*

This is a way of making a lei by winding a cord or string around flowers, leaves, and fruits to hold them to a center backing or to another cord.

The directions that follow will tell you how to make a *lei wili* to wear as a neck lei or a head lei.

WHAT YOU NEED

1. One or two large, fresh green ti leaves.
2. Long strips of hau fiber. Directions for preparing this are in section IV, 2. If you do not have hau fiber, you can use lengths of raffia or string. The amount of cord you need will depend on the length of your lei and the amount of plant material you use.

You can use almost any kind of flowers and leaves for your lei. Plan the pattern you want to use. Decide whether you want your lei to look full or dainty when you choose your plant material.

Trim the flower and leaf stems so that they are about two inches long. Put the stems into water for at least one hour. This will help to keep the plant material fresh.

It is better to have more flowers and leaves than you think you will use.

WHAT TO DO

1. Soak the hau fiber or the raffia for a few minutes before you use it. This will make it soft and easy to wind. The hau will stay damp and keep the lei fresh.
2. Debone the ti leaf. You can find directions for doing this in section I, 1. Trim the stem. Split the leaf in half by tearing from the tip end down to the stem end. Take one of the half ti leaves and fold it in half lengthwise so that it is one-half to three-fourths of an inch wide.
3. Decide how you will arrange your flowers and leaves as you make your lei.
4. Attach your cord to the folded leaf by knotting it about one inch from the tip end of the leaf.
5. Begin your lei by first placing a leaf or a small group of leaves against the ti leaf backing. Wind the cord around the stems one or two times. Pull the cord firmly, but not so tight that you cut the stems. Add more flowers and leaves by placing one or two at a time against the ti leaf backing. Wind the cord around them and the backing firmly once or twice.
6. To add more winding cord, hold one end of the new cord beside the first cord. Hold both of these ends together, make a loop, and push both ends through. Pull tightly.

65

What To Do: Steps 5, 6

MAKING A NECK LEI

1. To add another folded half ti leaf, put two or three inches of the tip end of the new leaf over the last two or three inches of the first leaf. Continue to add more flowers and leaves.

2. When the first half of your lei is long enough, end your winding. Do this by making a loop with the cord behind the lei backing. Then bring the cord end around to the front of the lei. Poke the cord end through the loop. Pull tightly. Make this kind of knot twice.

3. Trim the end of your lei so that you have three inches of ti leaf and ten inches of cord left.

4. Now make a second *lei wili* in the same way. Make it as long as the first one.

5. Overlap the two bare ti leaf ends as closely as possible. Use the cords to tie these overlapped ends together in a square knot.

6. Place more flowers and leaves on the bare backing. Hold them to the backing by winding with the cords. When the last of the plant material has been fastened onto the lei, knot the cords to hold everything in place. Trim any leftover cord.

Neck Lei: Step 2 (front view)

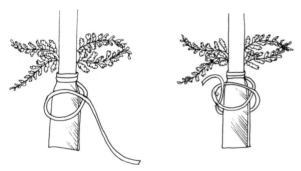

Neck Lei: Step 2 (back view)

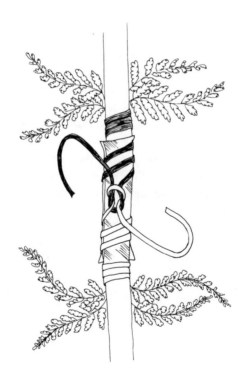

Neck Lei: Step 5

67

MAKING A HEAD LEI

1. Stop adding leaves and flowers when the lei goes around
   your head with two to three inches to spare. Hold the last
   of your leaves and flowers in place. Do this by making a
   loop with the cord behind the ti leaf. Bring the cord end
   around to the front of the lei. Poke the end of the cord
   through the loop. Pull tightly. Make this kind of knot
   twice.
2. Put the tip end of the lei over the stem end of the leaf.
   Wind the cord around the overlapped parts a few times.
   Try to hide the cord under the plant material as you wind
   it. Knot it tightly. Trim any leftover cord.

Keep your lei fresh by wrapping it in damp paper towels or
newspaper. Store it in a tightly closed plastic bag in the refrigerator.

When your lei is dry and brown, use the dried *pala'ā* ferns
to make dye. Directions for this are in section VIII, 9.

VII. LEIS AND LEI CARRIERS (NĀ LEI A ME NĀ MEA LAWE I LEI)

6. *Lei Hīpuʻu*

Hīpuʻu is a Hawaiian word for ''knot.'' No needle and thread are needed to make a *lei hīpuʻu* because the stems of leaves are knotted together to make a chain.

The directions below tell you how to make a *lei hīpuʻu* using kukui leaves. This lei is tied together at the back of your neck and is open at the bottom.

WHAT YOU NEED

About forty small or medium-sized kukui leaves. The stems of the leaves you pick should be four or more inches long.

WHAT TO DO

1. Put a leaf flat on a table with its underside down.
2. Tie a loose knot in the middle of the stem.
3. Put a second leaf on top of the first one with its underside down. Slip the second leaf stem into the knot. Pull the second stem through the knot as far as it will go.
4. Tighten the knot in the first stem.
5. Tie a loose knot at the middle of the second stem.
6. Slip a third leaf stem into this knot. Pull the third stem through the knot as far as it will go.
7. Tuck the end of the stem of the first leaf into this knot.
8. Tighten the knot.

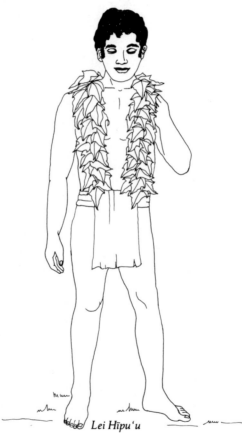

Lei Hīpuʻu

69

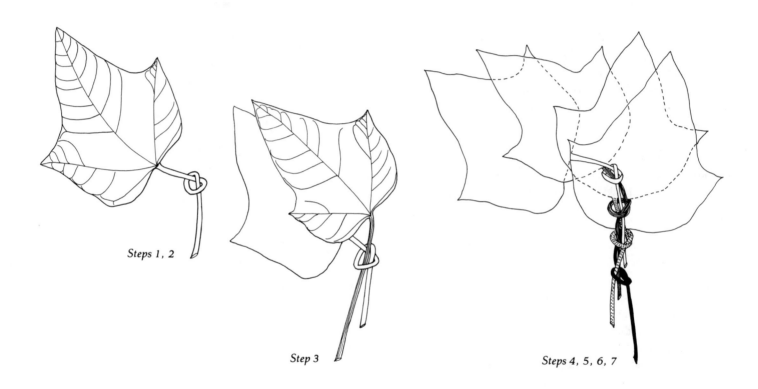

Steps 1, 2

Step 3

Steps 4, 5, 6, 7

70

9. Continue to add new leaves in the same way. Each time you make a knot and add a new leaf, tuck as many stem ends into the knot as you can. Pull the knot tight.

When the chain of kukui leaves is about twenty-four inches long, you have made half of the lei. Make the other half in exactly the same way. Join the two halves together:

1. Tie the last stems of the two halves together in a loose square knot.
2. Tuck any stem ends that are near the square knot into the knot.
3. Tighten the square knot.

A kukui leaf lei will last several days. You can help it last longer by putting it on a damp towel. Make sure the leaves are flat. Cover the lei with another damp towel. Keep the lei in a cool place.

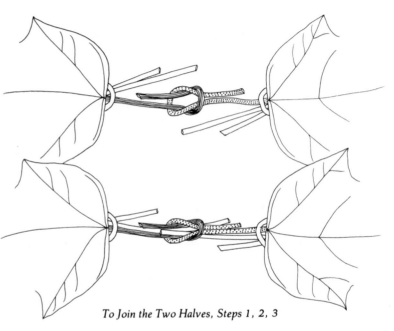

To Join the Two Halves, Steps 1, 2, 3

VII. LEIS AND LEI CARRIERS (NĀ LEI A ME NĀ MEA LAWE I LEI)
7. *Ti Leaf Lei Carrier #1 (Pū'olo)*

This kind of carrier is a good one for leis. It will keep a lei cool and fresh.

WHAT YOU NEED

1. About ten big, green ti leaves with long stems.
2. Two dried, brown ti leaves to use for tying.
3. Some string to use for tying in case you cannot pull the brown ti leaf ties tight enough.

WHAT TO DO

1. Take the bone out of each of the green ti leaves. Look in section I, 1 for directions for deboning ti leaves. If you want to have a firmer carrier, you can leave the bones in the ti leaves.
2. Put the green ti leaves shiny side down in a circle with their stems pointing toward the center. Your leaves will look like a wheel.
3. Bend the stems up in the middle of the wheel. Gather them together and tie them close to the beginning of the leaf part. Use a brown ti leaf or a string to tie the stems together tightly.
4. If your lei is untied you can wind it around the stems. If

Step 2

72

Step 3

Step 4

your lei is tied you can twist it over the stems several times.

5. To enclose the lei inside the carrier, bring the point of each leaf toward the stems one by one. Bring the inside leaves up first. Try to be sure each leaf overlaps the next one a little.

6. Tie the leaf tips together with the stems. Use a brown ti leaf to tie the carrier.

Step 6

74

VII. LEIS AND LEI CARRIERS (NĀ LEI A ME NĀ MEA LAWE I LEI)
8. *Ti Leaf Lei Carrier #2 (Pūʻolo)*

This carrier has a handle because you use the ti plant without taking the leaves off the stalk.

WHAT YOU NEED

1. A ti leaf stalk with many large green leaves near the top.
2. Brown ti leaves to use for tying.
3. Some string to tie the inside of the carrier tightly.

WHAT TO DO

1. Cut a ti stalk so that you have about two feet of the woody stem with green leaves at the top.
2. Turn the stalk upside-down. Tie the leaves tightly around the stalk. Tie them below their stems at the place where the leaves begin to be a little wider. This will make the stalk and leaves look a little like a broom.
3. Push down gently on the stalk to spread out the ti leaves. Pull the leaves to make a wheel around the stem.
4. Wind your lei around the stem. Next, bring the tip of each leaf up to the stem. Bring the inside leaves up first. Make sure each leaf overlaps the next one a little.

Steps 2, 3, 4

75

5. Tie the leaves around the stem close to their tips.
6. The newest leaf on the plant, the one still unfolded, will stick out of the carrier.
7. The woody stem of this carrier can be used to plant new ti plants. Look at section X, 6 for directions that will tell you how to do this.

Steps 5, 6

VII. LEIS AND LEI CARRIERS (NĀ LEI A ME NĀ MEA LAWE I LEI)
9. *Ti Leaf Lei Carrier #3 (Pū'olo)*

This lei carrier is used to hold small leis. You might use this package to carry a *lei hala* or a few strands of pakalana.

WHAT YOU NEED

1. A small lei.
2. Four or more fresh green ti leaves with long stems. The ti leaves should all be about the same size. The number you need will depend upon the size of your ti leaves and the size of your lei.
3. Two small green or brown ti leaves to tie your package. You could also use hau fiber cord for tying. Look at section IV, 2 for the directions for making this.

WHAT TO DO

1. Place one ti leaf on a flat surface, shiny side down.
2. Put your lei lengthwise on the leaf.
3. Put a second leaf, shiny side up, on top of your lei. Put the tip end of the second leaf over the stem end of the first leaf.
4. Continue to wrap your package with ti leaves until your lei is fully covered. Work with the shiny side of the leaf

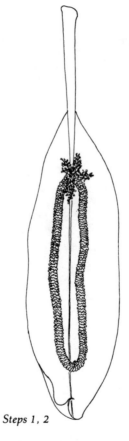

Steps 1, 2

facing out. Be sure to put a stem end next to a leaf tip as
you wrap.

5. Tie each end of your package with a small ti leaf or with
cord.

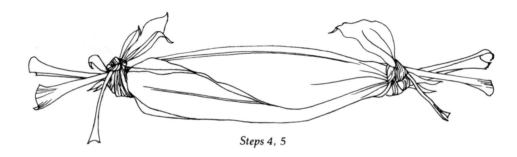

Steps 4, 5

VII. LEIS AND LEI CARRIERS (NĀ LEI A ME NĀ MEA LAWE I LEI)
10. *Ti Leaf Lei Carrier #4 (Pū'olo)*

This lei carrier holds the lightest, most delicate leis, such as a strand of pikake.

WHAT YOU NEED

1. An untied lei.
2. Two large, fresh green ti leaves.
3. A thirty-six- to forty-four-inch length of hau fiber cord, raffia cord, or string. Directions for stripping hau bark to get hau fiber are in section IV, 2.

WHAT TO DO

1. Debone the ti leaves. Directions for doing this are in section I, 1.
2. Put one ti leaf on a flat surface, shiny side down.
3. Coil your lei. Put it on the ti leaf about five inches from the tip of the leaf.
4. Fold the tip end of the ti leaf over the top of the lei. Bring the lower part of the ti leaf over the tip end. Wrap this lower part around the lei. Continue to wrap all the way to the stem end.
5. Lay your second ti leaf on a flat surface, shiny side down.
6. Put your wrapped lei on the second ti leaf about five inches from the tip of the leaf. Place it so that the open

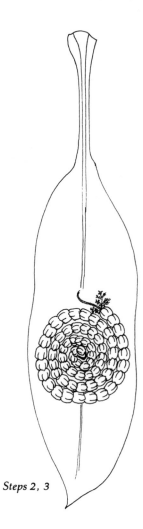

Steps 2, 3

79

ends of the package face the tip and stem ends of the second ti leaf.

7. Now fold the tip end of the second ti leaf over the top of the lei. Bring the lower part of the ti leaf over the tip end. Wrap this lower part around the lei. Continue to wrap all the way down to the stem end.

8. Use cord to tie your leaves like a package. Tie the package so that all four sides are held by cord.

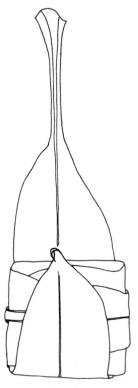

Step 7

Step 8

VII. LEIS AND LEI CARRIERS (NĀ LEI A ME NĀ MEA LAWE I LEI)
11. *Banana Stalk Lei Carrier (Hā Maiʻa)*

By following these directions you can make curved trays from a banana stalk in which to carry leis.

WHAT YOU NEED

1. A banana stalk from which the fruit has already been taken.
2. A saw to cut down the stalk.

WHAT TO DO

1. Cut down the banana stalk.
2. Cut off the top of the banana stalk.
3. Cut the stalk into the length of your leis.
4. Peel away the outside layer of the stalk.
5. Use the layers just under the outside layer for lei trays.

Banana sap makes stains that do not come out. Be careful when you work with banana plants.

Banana Stalk Lei Carrier

VIII. DYES (NĀ WAIHOʻOLUʻU)

Long ago people used parts of plants to make dyes. These pages have directions for making dyes from plant material. Hawaiians might have used these dyes to color their *kapa*, or tapa.

Before you try these dye recipes, you should know the following things:

1. Dyes made from plant material are usually not as bright as those made from chemicals. Usually they are pale. Sometimes they are dark.
2. The shades of dyes may be different each time you make dye. Some of the things that can change the shades of dyes are the amount of plant material you use, whether the plant material is young or old, the time of year you gather your plant material, whether the plant grows in the sun or shade, how long you let the cloth you are dyeing stay in the dye bath, and the kind of cloth you use.
3. Most plant material used in making dyes should be shredded, chopped, or torn into very small pieces. This will help you get as much color from the material as possible.
4. The dye recipes on the next pages are for coloring small pieces of cloth. You may want to print patterns on your cloth, too. You can use these dyes for printing, but before you do, you need to make them thicker. To do this, put the dye in a shallow pan in direct sunlight for a day or more. The fern dye is a good one to use for this.

Use Hawaiian paint brushes or bamboo stamps to print patterns. Directions for making brushes and stamps are in sections III, 2 and III, 3.

In the directions on the next pages plant material is sometimes heated on the stove. You can also get color from plant material without heating it by soaking it a longer time.

VIII. DYES (NĀ WAIHOʻOLUʻU)
1. *Turmeric Dye (ʻŌlena)*

The underground stem of the ʻōlena plant makes a yellow or gold dye. One of the Hawaiian words for yellow is ʻōlenalena.

ʻŌlena is a spice that is also called "turmeric." You can buy it from the spice shelf of a grocery store and use it to make dye instead of using fresh ʻōlena.

WHAT YOU NEED

1. About four tablespoons of turmeric.
2. About two cups of water.
3. Six-inch squares of nonfusible pellon. You can buy nonfusible pellon in any fabric store. It looks a little like *kapa*. Wash the pellon in soap and water and rinse it before you use it.
4. A tablespoon.
5. A measuring cup.
6. A heat-proof mixing bowl.
7. A piece of cloth about eight inches square made from an old white pillowcase or sheet.
8. A piece of string.
9. Waxed paper.

WHAT TO DO

1. Put the water into the bowl.

Turmeric Plant

83

2. Measure the turmeric and put it on the old white cloth. Use the string to tie the cloth closed to make a bag. Put it into the water.
3. Keep the bag in the water about twenty minutes. Squeeze the dye color out of the bag.
4. Take the bag of dye out of the water. Save it because you can use it again.
5. Put your pellon into the dye bath. Be sure the pellon is covered by the water. Stir it once in a while. Keep the pellon in the dye bath an hour or longer.
6. Dry your pellon in the shade. Dry it flat on a piece of waxed paper.

VIII. DYES (NĀ WAIHOʻOLUʻU)
2. Candlenut Bark Dye (ʻIli Kukui)

The inner bark of large, old kukui trees is a reddish color. You can make dye from chips of this inner bark.

WHAT YOU NEED

1. About one-fourth of a cup of reddish inner bark of the kukui tree cut into very small bits.
2. About one cup of water.
3. A six-inch square of nonfusible pellon. You can buy this in any fabric shop. It looks a little like *kapa*. Wash the pellon in soap and water and rinse it before you use it.
4. A measuring cup.
5. An enamel cooking pot with a lid.
6. A heat-proof mixing bowl.
7. An eight-inch piece of cheesecloth.
8. A piece of string.
9. Waxed paper.

WHAT TO DO

1. Peel or cut pieces of bark from a large kukui tree. Be careful to take only a little of the inner bark from a very large tree. Do not damage the tree.
2. Scrape or cut off the red inner bark and chop it into small pieces.
3. Put the small pieces of inner bark onto the cheesecloth. Use the string to tie it closed. Soak the bag in the water for twenty-four hours or longer. Press and squeeze it from time to time to get the dye color out of the bark.
4. Simmer the bag of bark pieces in the same water for one hour or longer. Cover the cooking pot with a lid as you do this.
5. Put your pellon into the reddish dye water. Simmer the dye and the pellon about one hour or more.
6. Remove the bag. Save the bag of bark pieces because you can use it again. Keep the pellon in the dye water until the water is cool, or longer if you want a deeper color.
7. Dry your dyed pellon in the shade. Dry it flat on a piece of waxed paper.

VIII. DYES (NĀ WAIHOʻOLUʻU)
3. *Candlenut Leaf Dye (Lau Kukui)*

Dye made from kukui leaves is a pale gray-green.

WHAT YOU NEED

1. About two cups of kukui leaves torn or cut into very small pieces. Press the leaf bits tightly into the measuring cup.
2. About two cups of water.
3. A six-inch square of nonfusible pellon. You can buy this in any fabric store. It looks a little like *kapa*. Wash the pellon in soap and water and rinse it before you use it.
4. A measuring cup.
5. An enamel cooking pot with a lid.
6. A strainer.
7. A heat-proof mixing bowl.
8. Waxed paper.

WHAT TO DO

1. Put two cups of kukui leaf bits into the water. Soak the leaf bits in the water overnight.
2. Simmer the leaves in the water about forty-five minutes. Cover the cooking pot with a lid as you do this.
3. Pour the dye water through the strainer into the mixing bowl.
4. Put your pellon into the water. Keep it there until the water is cool, or longer if you want a deeper color.
5. Dry your dyed pellon in the shade. Dry it flat on a piece of waxed paper.

VIII. DYES (NĀ WAIHOʻOLUʻU)
4. Candlenut Hull Dye (ʻIli Hua Kukui)

The dye made from the outer layer, or hull, of green kukui nuts makes a gray dye.

WHAT YOU NEED

1. About six green kukui nuts.
2. About one cup of water.
3. A six-inch square of nonfusible pellon. You can buy this in any fabric store. It looks a little like *kapa*. Wash the pellon in soap and water and rinse it before you use it.
4. A paring knife.
5. A measuring cup.
6. An enamel cooking pot with a lid.
7. A strainer.
8. A heat-proof mixing bowl.
9. Waxed paper.

WHAT TO DO

1. Peel or chip off the outer hull of the green kukui nuts. Cut them into very small pieces. You need enough hull pieces to make one full cup.
2. Soak the pieces of green hull in the water for three hours or longer. Squeeze the pieces of hull to get the color out of them.
3. Put the water and the hull pieces in the cooking pot on the stove. Cover the pot with a lid. Simmer the hull pieces for about thirty minutes.
4. Pour the dye water through the strainer into the mixing bowl.
5. Put your pellon into the dye water. Keep it there until the water is cool, or longer if you want a deeper color.
6. Dry your dyed pellon in the shade. Dry it flat on a piece of waxed paper.

VIII. DYES (NĀ WAIHO'OLU'U)
5. *Beach Naupaka Dye (Lau Naupaka Kahakai)*

Beach naupaka is a plant that grows along many Hawaiian beaches. It has only a half flower. Beach naupaka makes a pale yellow-green dye.

WHAT YOU NEED

1. About two cups of finely cut or torn mature beach naupaka leaves. Press the leaf bits tightly into the measuring cup.
2. About two cups of water.
3. A measuring cup.
4. A heat-proof mixing bowl.
5. A wooden spoon for stirring.
6. A strainer.
7. An enamel cooking pot with a lid.
8. A six-inch square of nonfusible pellon. You can buy it in any fabric store. It looks a little like *kapa*. Wash the pellon in soap and water and rinse it before you use it.
9. Waxed paper.

WHAT TO DO

1. Put two cups of beach naupaka leaf bits into the water. Soak the leaf bits in the water at least three hours or overnight.

88

Beach Naupaka Plant

2. Put the water and the leaf pieces in the cooking pot on the stove. Cover the pot with a lid. Simmer the water and leaf pieces about forty-five minutes. Stir them from time to time.
3. Pour the dye water through the strainer into the mixing bowl.
4. Put your pellon into the water. Keep it there until the water is cool, or longer if you want a deeper color.
5. Dry your dyed pellon in the shade. Dry it flat on a piece of waxed paper.

VIII. DYES (NĀ WAIHOʻOLUʻU)
6. Banana Leaf Dye (Lau Maiʻa)

Dye made from banana leaves is a pale green. Older banana leaves are darker than new ones and make a darker green dye.

WHAT YOU NEED

1. About two cups of banana leaves torn or cut into very small pieces. Press the leaf bits tightly into the measuring cup.
2. About two cups of water.
3. A six-inch square of nonfusible pellon. You can buy this in any fabric store. It looks a little like *kapa*. Wash your pellon in soap and water and rinse it before you use it.
4. A measuring cup.
5. An enamel cooking pot with a lid.
6. A strainer.
7. A heat-proof mixing bowl.
8. Waxed paper.

WHAT TO DO

1. Put two cups of banana leaf bits into the water. Soak the leaf bits in the water overnight.
2. Put the water and the leaf pieces in the cooking pot on the stove. Cover the pot with a lid. Simmer the water and leaf pieces about forty-five minutes.
3. Pour the dye water through the strainer into the mixing bowl.
4. Put your pellon into the water. Keep it there until the water is cool, or longer if you want a deeper color.
5. Dry your dyed pellon in the shade. Dry it flat on a piece of waxed paper.

VIII. DYES (NĀ WAIHOʻOLUʻU)
7. *Banana Flower Covering Dye (Liko Pua Maiʻa)*

This dye is usually a pale purple color. It is made from the purple skin of the banana flower buds.

WHAT YOU NEED

1. About one cup of small pieces of the purple banana flower covering.
2. About one cup of water.
3. A six-inch square of nonfusible pellon. You can buy this in any fabric shop. It looks a little like *kapa*. Wash your pellon in soap and water and rinse it before you use it.
4. A measuring cup.
5. A heat-proof mixing bowl.
6. An enamel cooking pot with a lid.
7. A strainer.
8. A wooden spoon.
9. Waxed paper.

WHAT TO DO

1. Peel the purple covering away from each set of flowers. Chop or cut it into small pieces.
2. Soak the pieces of the banana flower covering in the water overnight. Squeeze the pieces of the banana flower covering to get the color out of them.

Banana Flower Covering

91

3. Put them and the dye water in a pan on the stove. Cover the pan with a lid. Simmer them in the water about thirty minutes.
4. Pour the dye through the strainer into a bowl. Use the wooden spoon to press out as much color as possible.
5. Put your pellon into the hot dye water and soak it overnight.
6. Dry your pellon in a shady place. Dry it flat on a piece of waxed paper.

VIII. DYES (NĀ WAIHOʻOLUʻU)
8. *Male Inflorescence of the Breadfruit Tree Dye (ʻIli Pōule ʻUlu)*

The flower cluster, or male inflorescence, of the breadfruit tree turns brown and falls from the tree. Its covering makes a brown dye.

WHAT YOU NEED

1. About one cup of the outside layer of flower clusters.
2. About two cups of water.
3. A six-inch square of nonfusible pellon. You can buy this in any fabric store. It looks a little like *kapa*. Wash the pellon in soap and water and rinse it before you use it.
4. A measuring cup.
5. An enamel cooking pot with a lid.
6. An eight-inch piece of old white cloth.
7. A piece of string.
8. A wooden spoon.
9. Waxed paper.

WHAT TO DO

1. Scrape off the outside of the dried flower cluster. To get this material, scrape the flower clusters with an *ʻopihi* shell or knife.
2. Put about one cup of the scraped material on the old white cloth. Use the string to tie it closed.

3. Put the bag of dye material into the water in a covered pot on the stove. Simmer the water and plant material about thirty minutes.
4. Use the wooden spoon to press out as much dye as you can.
5. Put your pellon in the water. Keep it there until the water is cool, or longer if you want a deeper color.
6. Dry your pellon in a shady place. Dry it flat on a piece of waxed paper.

Male Inflorescence of the Breadfruit Tree

93

VIII. DYES (NĀ WAIHOʻOLUʻU)
9. *Fern Dye (Kupukupu)*

Very dry ferns make a brown dye. A good place to get dried ferns is from old leis. Save your leis that have *palaʻā* ferns in them. Dry the ferns until they are brown. Use them to make dye.

WHAT YOU NEED

1. About two cups of tightly packed dried fern pieces.
2. About one cup of water.
3. A six-inch square of nonfusible pellon. You can buy this in a fabric store. It looks a little like *kapa*. Wash the pellon in soap and water and rinse it before you use it.
4. A measuring cup.
5. An enamel cooking pot with a lid.
6. An eight-inch piece of cheesecloth.
7. A piece of string.
8. A wooden spoon.
9. Waxed paper.

WHAT TO DO

1. Cut or tear the dried fern into very small pieces.
2. Put the fern pieces onto the cheesecloth. Use the string to tie it closed.

Palaʻā Fern Plant

3. Put the bag of fern pieces and the water into the cooking pot. Cover the pot with a lid.

4. Simmer the bag of fern pieces in the water at least two hours.

5. Use the wooden spoon to press the bag against the side of the cooking pot to squeeze out the color.

6. Put your pellon in the dye water for about the last thirty minutes of simmering.

7. Take out the bag of fern pieces. Save the bag because you can use it a second time.

8. Keep your pellon in the dye water until the water is cool.

9. Dry your pellon in the shade. Dry it flat on a piece of waxed paper.

Dye made from dried *pala'ā* fern is a dark brown. It can be made thicker by putting it in a large, very shallow pan in the sun for a day or longer. This thicker dye is good to use for printing and painting.

IX. FOODS (NĀ MEAʻAI)
1. *How to Prepare Taro (Kalo)*

The Hawaiian name for taro is *kalo*. Long ago it was usually cooked in the *imu*, or underground steam oven.

The part of the taro that you see in grocery stores is the corm, or underground stem. It is not the root as many people think. The corm is very easy to cook.

WHAT YOU NEED

1. A covered pot large enough to hold the taro.
2. Enough water to cover the taro.
3. A knife or fork.
4. A bowl of cold water.
5. Taro corms.

WHAT TO DO

1. Wash the corms well.
2. Do not peel the taro. Just place it in a pot. Cover the taro with water.
3. Cover the pot. Bring the water to a boil over high heat.
4. Turn the heat down to medium.
5. Continue cooking until you can poke a knife or fork through the center very easily. If you eat taro that has not been cooked well, you will have a very itchy mouth.
6. Remove the taro from the pot. Put it into cold water. Then you will be able to peel it with your hands.

96

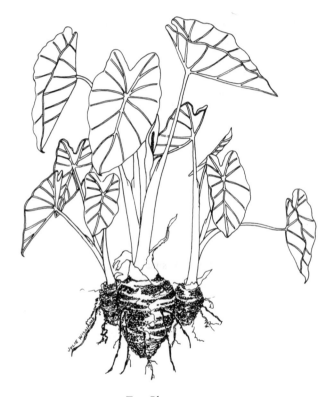

Taro Plant

IX. FOODS (NĀ MEA'AI)
2. Making Poi (Kalo)

Poi was very important to the people of old Hawai'i. People ate poi almost every day.

WHAT YOU NEED

1. Some cooked taro corms. Look in section IX, 1 to find directions for cooking taro.
2. Water in a dish.
3. A poi pounder and poi-pounding board. You could use a shallow, heavy pan and a potato masher.
4. A bowl.

WHAT TO DO

1. Break the cooked corms into pieces. Place a few on the board or in the pan.
2. Break the taro into very small pieces with the pounder. Wet your other hand. Slip it under the taro. Turn the taro over so that it will not stick to the board or pan.
3. When the taro is in small pieces, wet the bottom of the pounder or masher. Continue to mash and turn the taro until it is smooth and thick. Keep your hand and the pounder wet.
4. Scoop up this thick poi and place it in a bowl. Add a little water at a time. Mix it into the poi with your hand and fingers. Keep adding water a little at a time. Mix the water in until you have the poi as thick or as thin as you like to eat it.

IX. FOODS (NĀ MEA'AI)
3. *How to Prepare Sugar Cane (Kō)*

Hawaiians of long ago believed that chewing sugar cane made teeth strong and clean. They also chewed sugar cane while traveling so they would not get hungry. Sugar cane was eaten as a sweet, too.

Follow these directions to prepare some sugar cane.

WHAT YOU NEED

1. A stalk of sugar cane.
2. A sharp knife.

WHAT TO DO

1. Cut the sugar cane into pieces with a sharp knife. Cut the pieces between the internodes, or sections.
2. Stand each piece up. Carefully cut off the hard outer skin with the knife. You can also peel cane with your teeth.
3. Cut the cane into long strips.
4. Chew a strip of cane. Do not swallow the pulp. Just swallow the juice. Then take the pulp out of your mouth.

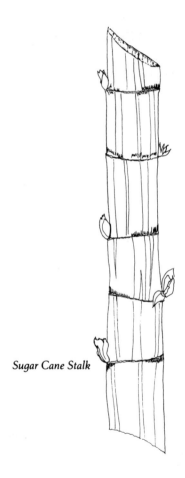

Sugar Cane Stalk

IX. FOODS (NĀ MEAʻAI)
4. *Lomi Salmon (Kāmano Lomi)*

The Hawaiian word *lomi* means to knead, or massage. This method of making lomi salmon was used to let the salt and other flavors blend together.

WHAT YOU NEED

1. A small pan.
2. Water.
3. Paper towels.
4. 4 small bowls.
5. A sharp knife and chopping board.
6. A serving bowl.
7. ¼ pound of salt salmon.
8. 3 medium size tomatoes, washed.
9. 2 stalks of green onions, washed.
10. 1 small, round onion, if you wish.

WHAT TO DO

1. Place the salmon in a small pan. Cover it with water. Let it stand for an hour or so. *Lomi*, or knead, it every so often with a clean hand to remove the extra salt. Change the water whenever you knead the salmon.
2. Throw out the water. Rinse the fish with fresh water. Pat it dry with paper towels.
3. Cut the salmon into very small pieces. Put them into a bowl.
4. Cut the tomatoes into very small pieces. Put them into a bowl.
5. Cut the green onions into ¼-inch pieces. Put them into another bowl.
6. Peel the round onion. Cut it into very small pieces. Store them in another bowl.
7. Cover all the bowls of food. Place them in the refrigerator.
8. When you are ready to serve, mix the salmon, tomatoes, and round onion together. Sprinkle the green onions over the top.
9. Be sure to serve this dish very cold. It tastes good with poi.

IX. FOODS (NĀ MEA'AI)
5. *Fish Wrapped in Ti Leaves (Lāwalu)*

Hawaiians of long ago wrapped their fish in ti leaves before placing it on coals to cook. This is an easy recipe for you to try.

WHAT YOU NEED

1. A fat mullet or any white-fleshed fish, cleaned.
2. Hawaiian salt.
3. Four or more large, fresh green ti leaves with long stems.
4. Warm coconut milk.

WHAT TO DO

1. If you are using an oven, preheat it to 350°F. If you are using coals, start the fire.
2. Rinse the cleaned fish. Rub it with Hawaiian salt inside and out.
3. Debone two ti leaves. Directions for doing this are in section I, 1.
4. Put a ti leaf with a midrib on a flat surface, shiny side up. Lay your cleaned fish on this leaf.
5. Lay a second ti leaf with a midrib, shiny side down, over the fish. Put the stem end of this ti leaf over the tip of the first leaf.
6. Tuck the sides of the top leaf under the fish.
7. Wind one deboned ti leaf around the bundle. Wind from the tip end of the top leaf down to the stem end.
8. Wind the other deboned ti leaf around the bundle. Wind from the stem end of the top leaf down to the tip end.
9. Tie each deboned stem end in a knot around the bundle. Make the knots as close as you can to the fish.
10. If you use your oven, place the bundle in a roasting pan. Add a little water so the bundle will steam and bake.
11. If you use coals, just put the bundle directly on them. You may want to wind your bundle with a few more deboned ti leaves so the fish will not burn.
12. Allow about 20 minutes of cooking for each pound of fish.
13. Open the bundle and serve the fish. You may want to pour warm coconut milk over the fish before you serve it.

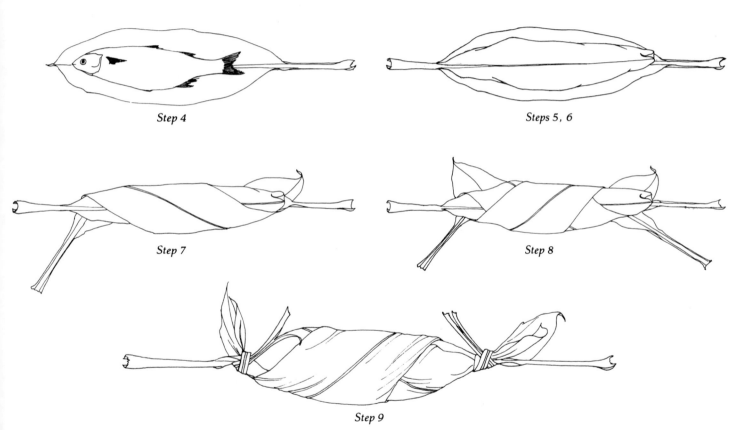

Step 4

Steps 5, 6

Step 7

Step 8

Step 9

6. *Kukui Nut Relish (ʻInamona)*

ʻ*Inamona* is used as a relish with raw seafood and with raw beef liver. Do not eat too much of it, though. It can make you sick if you eat a lot.

WHAT YOU NEED

1. Kukui nuts that have fallen from the tree, about thirty-five or more.
2. A bowl of water.
3. A shallow roasting pan.
4. A hammer.
5. A knife and chopping board.
6. Hawaiian salt.
7. A container for storage.
8. A bucket of water.
9. A screwdriver or something fairly sharp to help husk the kukui nuts.
10. Cookie sheets.

WHAT TO DO

1. The outer layer of the kukui nut is fairly soft. Poke the screwdriver into it and scrape off some of it. You can then pull the rest of the outer layer off quite easily. The middle layer also comes off easily. Take this off, too.

2. Put the nuts into a bowl of water. If the nuts have no kernels inside, they will float to the top right away. Throw these nuts away. Clean off the nuts that are left.

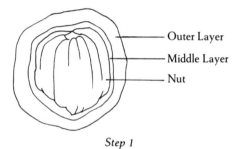

Outer Layer
Middle Layer
Nut

Step 1

3. Set the nuts in one layer on cookie sheets. Put them in the sun to dry. This will take about one day.
4. Set your oven to 300°F. Place the nuts in a roasting pan. Put the pan into the oven for about 1½ to 2 hours. Turn the nuts from time to time. When the nuts are dark brown, they are ready. If the nuts are not baked long enough, they will spoil quickly.
5. When the nuts are brown enough, remove them from the oven. Empty them into a bucket of cold water. In about ten minutes or so you will hear a crackling sound.
6. When the crackling sound stops, remove the nuts from the water.
7. Use the hammer to crack open the nuts. The softer inside kernels will fall out. You could also try to crack the nuts by holding one in each hand and hitting them together.
8. Chop a few kernels at a time into small bits. Put these small bits into a container. Continue to do this until all the kernels are finely chopped.
9. Add a little Hawaiian salt to the chopped kernels.
10. Stir the salt and the chopped kukui nut kernels together. Eat just a little with some fish, octopus, crab, or other food.

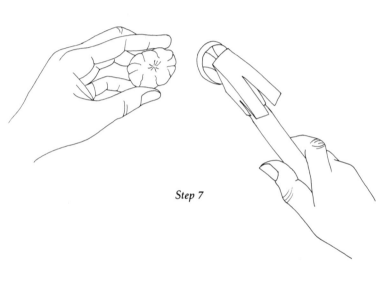

Step 7

103

IX. FOODS (NĀ MEAʻAI)
7. *Baked Banana (Maiʻa Kālua)*

The Hawaiians of long ago cooked bananas in the *imu*, an underground steam oven. You can cook them, too, using your oven.

WHAT YOU NEED

1. 2 or 3 cooking bananas.
2. A pan.

WHAT TO DO

1. Preheat the oven to 350°F.
2. Place the unpeeled bananas in the pan with a little water. Bake them for about 30 minutes until you can poke them easily with a fork, or until the skins begin to break.
3. Peel and eat them.
4. You may sprinkle sugar, lemon juice, and cinnamon on the baked and peeled bananas for a different taste.
5. If you use bananas that are a little green, you may peel them before baking.

IX. FOODS (NĀ MEA'AI)
8. *Baked Breadfruit ('Ulu Kālua)*

The Hawaiians used different parts of the breadfruit tree for different things. The fruit was used as food. However, it was not as important to them as taro and sweet potato.

Breadfruit was baked in an underground steam oven, or *imu*. You can use your oven to follow this easy recipe.

WHAT YOU NEED

1. A ripe breadfruit. A ripe breadfruit is soft and the outside skin is partly brown in color. You can see a white liquid oozing out near the stem.
2. A pan just big enough to hold the breadfruit. The pan should have about one-half inch of water in it so the breadfruit will not burn.
3. A knife and fork.
4. Butter.
5. Salt and pepper, or sugar.

WHAT TO DO

1. Preheat the oven to 350°F.
2. Wash the breadfruit. Poke it in several places with a fork. Put it into the pan with the water.
3. Bake for one hour.
4. Take the breadfruit from the oven.
5. Cut out or pull out the core and the stem.
6. Cut the breadfruit in half.
7. Spread each half with butter. Then sprinkle each half with salt and pepper. Or you may sprinkle sugar on the halves instead.

IX. FOODS (NĀ MEA'AI)
9. *Sweet Potato Pudding (Kō'elepālau)*

This Hawaiian dessert is very easy to make. It is good to eat, too.

WHAT YOU NEED

1. About 2 pounds of sweet potatoes.
2. A covered pot large enough to hold the sweet potatoes.
3. Enough water to cover the sweet potatoes.
4. 1½ cups of coconut milk, warmed.
5. A knife or fork.
6. A bowl and potato masher.
7. Clean ti leaf squares.

WHAT TO DO

1. Scrub the sweet potatoes clean.
2. Bring the pot of water to a boil over high heat. Put the sweet potatoes into the pot, cover, and turn the heat to medium.
3. Cook the sweet potatoes about 25 minutes, or until they can be poked easily with a knife or fork.
4. Peel the sweet potatoes while they are still warm.
5. Mash them in a bowl with the potato masher.
6. Add the coconut milk. Blend it into the sweet potatoes well.
7. Serve the pudding warm. Serve it on ti leaf squares.

IX. FOODS (NĀ MEAʻAI)
10. *Coconut Pudding (Haupia)*

Haupia is a coconut pudding. It is eaten as a dessert. The Hawaiians used *pia*, or arrowroot, to thicken this pudding. We use cornstarch instead today.

WHAT YOU NEED

1. Measuring cups.
2. Measuring spoons.
3. A pot. Use a nonstick one if you have it.
4. A wooden spoon for stirring.
5. An eight-inch square pan.
6. A knife.
7. Clean ti leaves, cut into squares.
8. 3 cups of coconut milk. If you are using frozen coconut milk, thaw it first.
9. ½ cup of sugar.
10. ½ cup of cornstarch.
11. ¼ teaspoon of salt.

WHAT TO DO

1. Put the cornstarch, sugar, and salt into the pot.
2. Slowly add the coconut milk to make a smooth liquid. Stir as you add the milk to get out all the lumps.
3. Put the pot on the stove. Turn the stove to medium heat. Keep stirring until the coconut milk boils.
4. Turn the stove down to low heat. Keep stirring and cooking until the mixture thickens.
5. Pour the mixture into a square pan. Chill it until it is firm.
6. Cut the pudding into two-inch squares. Serve on the clean ti leaf squares.

IX. FOODS (NĀ MEA'AI)
11. *Food Drying Bag*

The ancient Hawaiians made long ocean trips in their double-hulled canoes. Fresh food would have spoiled easily so most of the food they took had to be cooked and then dried. This would keep the food good to eat for a long time. On the following pages are recipes for dried foods. You need a drying rack for both recipes. If you do not have a drying rack, you can use the following directions to make your own simple drying bag.

WHAT YOU NEED

1. An eight- or nine-inch foil pie plate.
2. A round cake rack that fits inside the pie plate.
3. A knife or a large nail.
4. A thirty-inch square of fine mesh fiberglass screen.
5. A thirty-six-inch piece of strong string.
6. Some large paper clips.
7. The slices of food that you are going to dry.

WHAT TO DO

1. Use the knife or the nail to poke holes all over the bottom of the pie plate.
2. Put the cake rack into the pie plate.
3. Put the slices of food on the cake rack so that the slices do not touch each other.
4. Pull the four corners of the screen together to make the bag.
5. Wind the string tightly around the top of the screen bag several times and tie a double knot. Center the pie pan in the bag so that it does not tip to one side when the bag is lifted up.
6. Now you need to close the four open seams of the bag. To do this, fold one seam over itself once. Keep it closed with two large paper clips.
7. Close the other seams in the same way.
8. Hang your bag in direct sunlight above the ground. Be sure to bring your drying bag inside at night or when it rains.

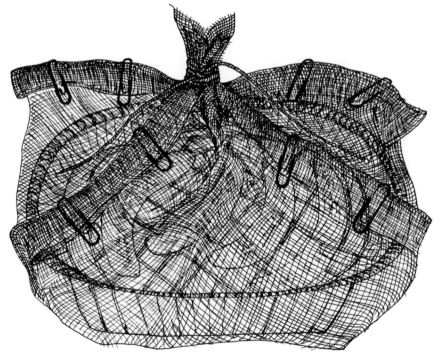

Food Drying Bag

IX. FOODS (NĀ MEAʻAI)
12. *Dried Banana (Maiʻa Pīkaʻo)*

WHAT YOU NEED

1. Ripe bananas.
2. A knife.
3. A drying rack or a drying bag. The directions for making a simple drying bag are in section IX, 11.

WHAT TO DO

1. Peel the bananas. Slice each of them into three or four long strips.
2. Lay the slices in a single layer on a drying rack. If you are using a drying bag, put them on the cake rack. Put the rack or bag in direct sunlight. Be sure to bring it inside at night or when it rains.
3. Turn the slices once a day. The slices will take four to fourteen days to dry. The length of time it takes will depend on where you dry them. Bananas will dry best in hot, sunny areas. The banana slices will change color as they dry.

IX. FOODS (NĀ MEA'AI)
13. *Dried Sweet Potato ('Uala Pīka'o)*

WHAT YOU NEED

1. Sweet potatoes.
2. A knife and fork.
3. A drying rack or simple drying bag. Directions for making a simple drying bag are in section IX, 11.

WHAT TO DO

1. Steam or boil the sweet potatoes until they are done. You can tell that they are ready when they can be poked easily with a fork.
2. Peel the sweet potatoes while they are still warm.
3. Let the sweet potatoes cool. Slice them into one-half-inch thick pieces.
4. Lay the slices in a single layer on a drying rack or on the cake rack in the pie plate of the drying bag. Put the rack or drying bag in direct sunlight. Remember to bring it inside at night or when it rains.
5. Turn the slices once each day. The slices should be ready in three or four days.

14. *Dried Yam ('Uhi Pīka'o)*

You can also prepare dried yam the same way as dried sweet potato.

Sweet Potato Plant

X. PLANTING (KANU)
1. *Coconut (Niu)*

There were many uses for the coconut in old Hawaiʻi. You can find ways to use parts of the coconut tree in many sections of this book.

HOW TO START

When coconuts fall from the tree they often sprout right where they land. You can use a sprouted nut to start a tree. You can also plant an unsprouted nut in which you can hear liquid sloshing when you shake it.

HOW TO PLANT

Soak an unsprouted nut in water for about three days before you plant it. Soaking will make the nut sprout faster. Dig a shallow hole in the ground. Put the coconut on its side in the hole and cover only the bottom two-thirds of the nut with soil.

Water the nut very well about twice a week. In about three months, or less, roots will push down into the soil and leaves will begin to grow.

A coconut can be started in a large container also.

HEIGHT

A coconut tree can grow to be seventy to one hundred feet tall.

Coconut

ENVIRONMENT

A coconut tree needs to be watered often after you first plant it. After it begins to sprout you may water it a little less often. Coconut trees grow well in many places, but they do best near the beach.

OTHER INFORMATION

Many varieties of coconut will take ten years from seed to fruit. Some will bear fruit for one hundred years.

In old Hawai'i the sprouted nut of a coconut tree was planted in a hole with an octopus. Hawaiians believed that the young coconut tree would then have strong and spreading roots like the arms of the octopus and that the nuts from the tree would be large and round like the head of the octopus. Usually coconuts were planted in groups of three.

X. PLANTING (KANU)
2. *Banana (Mai'a)*

There were at least seventy different kinds of bananas in old Hawai'i.

Hawaiians ate bananas both cooked and raw. You can find recipes that use bananas in sections IX, 7 and IX, 12.

HOW TO START

Bananas have suckers, or side shoots, near the bottom of mature plants. Look for a side shoot that is about six inches high. Cut it from the main stalk. Let the cut end of the side shoot dry for a few days before you plant it.

HOW TO PLANT

Bananas should be planted in a hole that is about two feet wide and one foot deep. Put compost, decayed plant material, mixed with soil and fertilizer in the hole. Fertilize the plant about two or three times a year.

HEIGHT

Some bananas grow to be about fifteen feet high. Others grow as tall as twenty or twenty-five feet.

Banana

ENVIRONMENT

Bananas grow well in most places in Hawai'i. They grow best where the ground is moist. Sometimes Hawaiians planted them near taro patches where there was water.

Bananas do best in full sun. They will grow in a little shade, too. High winds can tear banana leaves and push over the plant, so plant bananas where they are protected from the wind.

When new side shoots begin to grow, cut some of them away so that the main plant will get enough food and water.

You can get fruit from a banana plant in about one year. Each stalk bears fruit only once. Cut down the stalk after it has produced fruit.

OTHER INFORMATION

In old Hawai'i, people planted bananas when the sun was directly overhead and after they had eaten ripe bananas. They believed this would help the plant produce full, large fruit. They chose a side shoot from the side of the parent plant where the bunch of bananas was hanging.

The banana plant was sometimes used to represent the human body in spear throwing practice.

Sometimes dried banana leaves were made into sandals.

Hawaiians used pieces of banana stalks in their *imu* to make steam.

You could use banana stalks to make lei carriers. Directions for doing this are in section VII, 11.

Dye can be made from the leaf of the banana plant and the purple flower covering. There are directions for making these dyes in section VIII, 6 and VIII, 7.

X. PLANTING (KANU)
3. *Breadfruit ('Ulu)*

It is believed that breadfruit was brought to Hawai'i by the early Polynesians. Breadfruit is mentioned in very old legends.

There is a recipe for baked breadfruit in section IX, 8.

HOW TO START

The roots of breadfruit trees sprout shoots. These are used to start new trees. Find a shoot about six inches high. Cut the root on either side of the young plant. After several weeks this will grow new roots. Carefully dig up the new plant with its roots and the soil around them.

HOW TO PLANT

Plant the shoot about six to eight inches deep or as deep as you found it. Dig the hole large enough so that you can put some compost, decayed plant material, in it to help the new plant grow.

Hawaiians of long ago planted breadfruit on ''the last breath of the moon,'' or when the moon was becoming very small.

Breadfruit

HEIGHT

A breadfruit tree can grow to be sixty feet tall. It spreads out as it grows. Be sure you plant it where it will have plenty of room to grow.

ENVIRONMENT

Breadfruit grows best in wet valleys. It does not need much care if it is planted in a place where it has plenty of water and some sunshine.

Trees begin to bear fruit in about five to seven years. Fruits ripen between June and September. Pick the fruit when the skin turns brownish.

OTHER INFORMATION

The white sap of the breadfruit tree is sticky and was used as a glue in old Hawai'i. Bird catchers put it on tree branches to catch small birds.

The leaf sheath of the breadfruit tree was used for sand-paper when it was brown and dry and had fallen from the tree.

People used the wood of the breadfruit tree to make drums, surfboards, and poi-pounding boards.

X. PLANTING (KANU)
4. *Sugar Cane (Kō)*

In old Hawai'i there were more than thirty different kinds of sugar cane.

HOW TO START

Cut a mature stalk of sugar cane. Strip off the leaves. Cut the stalk into pieces about two feet long. These pieces are called the seed cane.

HOW TO PLANT

Hawaiians of long ago grew cane in clumps on mounds rather than in rows.

To plant sugar cane, lay the seed cane flat in a trough about six to eight inches deep. The trough should be a little longer than the length of stalk you have cut. Water the seed cane very well.

HEIGHT

Sugar cane is a giant form of grass and can grow three feet in three or four months. It can grow to be thirty feet tall. As cane grows it sheds old leaves from the bottom and grows new ones on top. When it is about ten feet tall, the stalk will begin to bend along the ground.

Sugar Cane

ENVIRONMENT

Sugar cane needs lots of water. You should water it very well every day. Plant the seed cane where it will have lots of sunshine all day. The leaves of the cane use the water and sun to form the sugar that is stored in the stalk. Sugar cane is harvested when the plant is about two years old and before the tassel appears.

OTHER INFORMATION

It is believed that Hawaiians brought sugar cane with them when they first came to the islands.

In old Hawai'i stalks of sugar cane were carried on long trips to chew for refreshment and energy. Sugar cane was used to sweeten foods and to make medicine taste better. Chewing the fibers cleaned the teeth. Directions for preparing sugar cane for chewing are in section IX, 3.

Sometimes the leaves of the cane were used to cover the inside walls of houses. Cane was planted around gardens as a windbreak.

X. PLANTING (KANU)
5. *Candlenut (Kukui)*

Kukui is one of the Hawaiian words for ''light.'' There are directions for making a kukui nut candle in section III, 1.

HOW TO START

Kukui nuts sprout easily if they have plenty of water. When you are hiking you can often find nuts that have rolled down into streams and have sprouted. You can use a sprouted nut to start a new tree. You can also start trees using brown, mature nuts. Scarify, or deeply scratch, them. This will help the nuts to absorb water. Soak the scratched nuts in water one or two days before you plant them.

HOW TO PLANT

You may start your kukui tree in a pot of rich, moist soil. Put each nut in its own pot. Put the nuts just below the surface of the soil and not too deep. When a plant is six to eight inches high, plant it in the ground.

HEIGHT

Sometimes kukui trees grow as tall as ninety feet. More often they are about fifty feet tall. Plant your kukui tree where it will have plenty of room to grow.

Kukui

ENVIRONMENT

Kukui are the trees with silvery-green leaves that you see when you look up into the mountains of Hawaiʻi. Kukui trees grow well in the mountains where there is plenty of water.

OTHER INFORMATION

In old Hawaiʻi people believed that you should not plant a kukui tree in front of your house. They believed you should ask a stranger to plant the tree for you.

The kukui tree had many uses. Besides using the nuts for candles, people also used parts of the kukui tree for dyes, leis, food, and medicine.

The leaves of the kukui tree vary from tree to tree. Some leaves look like the head of a pig. Some people say this is like the head of Kamapuaʻa, the pig demi-god.

X. PLANTING (KANU)
6. *Ti (Kī or Lāʻī)*

There were many uses for ti leaves in old Hawaiʻi. You can find out about some of them in several sections of this book.

HOW TO START

Ti plants can be started by cutting the woody stem into pieces twelve inches or longer. Cuttings from the part of the stalk near the top of the plant are easier to start than cuttings of older wood. A cutting of about six to eight inches of woody stem that has a cluster of leaves will root quickly in water and become a plant in six months.

HOW TO PLANT

Cuttings planted straight up will grow into single plants. Cuttings placed on their sides will grow into several plants.

To plant a twelve-inch ti cutting on its side, first remove the leaves. Place the cutting in a trough about four inches deep and about fourteen inches long. Give the plant some fertilizer about twice a year and water it very well.

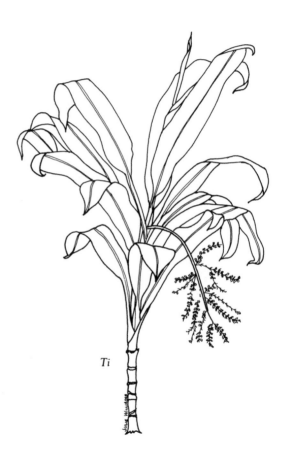

Ti

HEIGHT

Ti grows fast. It can grow to be twelve feet tall.

When you cut the ti stalk, new branches will grow from the buds below the place you cut.

ENVIRONMENT

Ti plants need lots of water. Well-watered plants will grow more quickly and have large leaves.

Ti plants will grow in the sun, but they grow better in shade. The leaves of the plant will be darker if the plant is grown in some shade.

OTHER INFORMATION

In old Hawai'i people believed that ti leaves would help keep evil spirits away. Many people still plant ti leaves near their houses for protection.

Ti leaves were used to wrap food and to make raincapes, sandals, and leis.

The tightly curled newest leaf in the center of the cluster of leaves was used as a bandage.

Pronunciation Guide for Hawaiian Words

In Hawai'i, increasing concern is being heard about the mispronunciation of Hawaiian words. In this book, we have supplied the diacritics necessary to the correct pronunciation of the words. The following guides (adapted from the *Hawaiian Dictionary*) are offered as an additional aid.

CONSONANTS

p, k	about as in English but with less aspiration.
h, l, m, n	about as in English.
w	after *i* and *e* usually like *v*; after *u* and *o* usually like *w*; initially and after *a* like *v* or *w*.
'	a glottal stop, similar to the sound between the *oh*'s in English *oh-oh*.

VOWELS

Unstressed

a	like *a* in above
e	like *e* in bet
i	like *y* in city
o	like *o* in sole
u	like *oo* in moon

Stressed

Vowels marked with macrons are somewhat longer than other vowels.

a, ā	like *a* in far		i, ī	like *ee* in see
e	like *e* in bet		o, ō	like *o* in sole
ē	like *ay* in play		u, ū	like *oo* in moon

DIPHTHONGS

These are always stressed on the first member,
but the two members are not as closely joined as in English.

ei, eu, oi, ou, ai, ae, ao, au

Bibliography

Beckwith, Martha. *Kepelino's Traditions of Hawaii.* Bishop Museum Bulletin No. 95; Honolulu, 1932.

Bryan, E. J., Jr. *Ancient Hawaiian Life.* Tongg Publishing Co.; Honolulu, 1950.

Buck, Peter H. *Arts and Crafts of Hawaii.* Bishop Museum Special Publication; Honolulu, 1945.

Dickey, Lyle. *String Figures From Hawaii.* Bishop Museum Bulletin No. 54; Honolulu, 1928.

Explorations: Ho'omāka'ika'i. The Kamehameha Schools; Honolulu, 1980.

Fornander, Abraham. *Hawaiian Antiquities and Folklore.* Bishop Museum Memoir, Vol. VI, No. 1; Honolulu, 1919.

Handy, E. S. C. *The Hawaiian Planter.* Bishop Museum Bulletin No. 161, Vol. I; Honolulu, 1940.

Handy, E. S. C., Elizabeth G. Handy, and Mary Kawena Pukui. *Native Planters in Old Hawaii: Their Life, Lore, and Environment.* Bishop Museum Bulletin No. 233; Honolulu, 1972.

Hawaiiana: A Handbook For Scouts. Aloha Council: Boy Scouts of America; Honolulu, 1973.

Hawaii's Sugar Islands. Hawaiian Sugar Planters' Association; Honolulu, 1974.

Hazama, Dorothy. *The Ancient Hawaiians: Who Were They? How Did They Live?* Hogarth Press; Honolulu, 1974.

Kaeppler, Adrienne L. *Kapa: Hawaiian Bark Cloth.* Boom Books; Hilo, 1980.

Krauss, Beatrice H. *Ethnobotany of Hawaii.* Department of Botany, University of Hawaii; Honolulu, 1972.

Krauss, Beatrice H. *Ethnobotany of the Hawaiians.* Harold L. Lyon Arboretum Lecture No. 5, University of Hawaii; Honolulu, 1974.

Krochmal, Arnold and Connie Krochmal. *The Complete Illustrated Book of Dyes From Natural Sources.* Doubleday and Co., Inc.; New York, 1974.

Krohn, Val Frieling. *Hawaii Dye Plants and Dye Recipes.* University of Hawaii Press; Honolulu, 1978.

Lindo, Cecelia K. and Nancy A. Mower (editors). *Polynesian Seafaring Heritage.* The Kamehameha Schools and the Polynesian Voyaging Society; Honolulu, 1980.

Lowe, Ruby Hasegawa. *Hawaiian Plants: Background and Activities.* Unpublished master's thesis, University of Hawaii; Honolulu, 1978.

Malo, David. *Hawaiian Antiquities.* Bishop Museum Special Publication No. 2; Honolulu, 1951.

McDonald, Marie A. *Ka Lei: The Leis of Hawaii.* Topgallant Publishing Company; Honolulu, 1979.

Miller, Carey D., Katherine Bazore, and Mary Bartow. *Fruits of Hawaii.* University of Hawaii Press; Honolulu, 1936.

Mitchell, Donald D. K. *Hawaiian Games For Today.* The Kamehameha Schools Press; Honolulu, 1975.

Mitchell, Donald D. K. *Resource Units In Hawaiian Culture.* The Kamehameha Schools Press; Honolulu, 1969, 1982.

Neal, Marie C. *In Gardens of Hawaii.* Bishop Museum; Honolulu, 1965.

Pukui, Mary Kawena and Samuel H. Elbert. *Hawaiian Dictionary: Hawaiian-English, English-Hawaiian.* University of Hawaii Press; Honolulu, 1957.

Pukui, Mary Kawena. ''Games of My Hawaiian Childhood.'' *California Folklore Quarterly*, Vol. II, No. 3, 1943.

Taylor, Clarice. *Hawaiian Almanac.* Tongg Publishing Company; Honolulu, 1957.

Titcomb, Margaret. *The Ancient Hawaiians: How They Clothed Themselves.* Hogarth Press; Honolulu, 1974.

Titcomb, Margaret. *Native Use of Fish in Hawaii.* The University Press of Hawaii; Honolulu, 1972.

Wichman, Juliet Rice. *Hawaiian Planting Traditions.* Honolulu Star-Bulletin; Honolulu, 1931.

Wilcox, Barbara Stevens, Susan G. Monden, and Herb Kawainui Kane. *The Kahuku Sugar Mill Story.* Island Heritage; Honolulu, 1975.

Williams, Julie Stewart. *Ancient Hawaiian Plant Dyes.* Unpublished manuscript; Honolulu, 1979.

Yee, Warren. ''Ti Culture.'' Agriculture Extension Circular No. 344, University of Hawaii; Honolulu, 1954.

About the Authors

Jane Abernethy has a Bachelor of Arts degree in sociology from the College of Wooster and a Master of Arts degree in education from the University of Pennsylvania. She has a graduate certificate in the psychology of reading from Temple University and has done additional graduate work at New York University, Columbia University, and the University of Hawaii. Miss Abernethy teaches English as a second language in Hawaii and Japan.

Suelyn Ching Tune graduated from Punahou School. She received a Bachelor of Arts degree from Occidental College in comparative literature and has a Master of Arts degree from New York University in educational psychology in reading. She completed a professional certificate in education at California State College at Los Angeles and has done additional graduate work at the University Of Hawaii, Brigham Young University (Hawaii campus), and New York University. Mrs. Tune teaches in The Kamehameha Schools Intermediate Reading Program.

Julie Stewart Williams graduated from The Kamehameha Schools and has a Bachelor of Education degree from the University of Hawaii, where she also received a Fifth Year Certificate. She earned a Master of Science degree in reading from St. Francis College in Fort Wayne, Indiana, and she completed additional graduate work at Indiana University and the University of Hawaii. Mrs. Williams is director of The Kamehameha Schools Intermediate Reading Program.